"Readers and listeners c [...] things, and customs that are only vaguely understood. Since many of them appear so often, Bibles may explain them in a footnote the first time they appear in a text, but then it becomes difficult for the reader to find the passage where the footnote first occurred. George Martin's book provides a very handy reference to those common names and customs as an ongoing aid to every Bible reader."

— *Father Mitch Pacwa, S.J.*

"This resource is an essential addition to the library of those beginning to delve into Scripture or looking to deepen their understanding. Written in accessible question-and-answer format and well-indexed, this helpful book provides the background needed to enter more fully into the world of the Bible and more clearly understand its saving message."

— *Mary Elizabeth Sperry, author of* Bible Top Tens

"George Martin has done us all a great service by pulling together all the background information that adds color, sound, and depth to the reading of the New Testament. It's clear, informative, and unrelentingly interesting! Now I have a single volume to recommend to Bible readers looking to flesh out their understanding of the Gospels."

— *Dr. John Bergsma, Professor of Theology at Franciscan University of Steubenville*

"George Martin has helped readers encounter Jesus through the Gospels and experience Scripture as God's word for many decades. This new assembly of articles is as fresh and informative as ever. Bridging solid biblical scholarship and rich spiritual nourishment, this collection illumines the shadows in the world of Jesus to help readers better understand his message."

— *Stephen J. Binz, biblical scholar and award-winning author*

# SCRIPTURE FOOTNOTES
The World of Jesus

# SCRIPTURE FOOTNOTES

## The World of Jesus

**GEORGE MARTIN**

Our
Sunday
Visitor

www.osv.com
Our Sunday Visitor Publishing Division
Our Sunday Visitor, Inc.
Huntington, Indiana 46750

This book contains material from the books *Bringing the Gospel of Mark to Life, Bringing the Gospel of Matthew to Life, Bringing the Gospel of Luke to Life,* and *Bringing the Gospel of John to Life,* all copyright © George Martin, published by Our Sunday Visitor.

Every reasonable effort has been made to determine copyright holders of excerpted materials and to secure permissions as needed. If any copyrighted materials have been inadvertently used in this work without proper credit being given in one form or another, please notify Our Sunday Visitor in writing so that future printings of this work may be corrected accordingly.

Our Sunday Visitor Publishing Division, Our Sunday Visitor, Inc., 200 Noll Plaza, Huntington, IN 46750; 1-800-348-2440.

ISBN: 978-1-68192-116-7 (Inventory No. T1846)
eISBN: 978-1-68192-117-4
LCCN: 2017951882

Cover design: Lindsey Riesen
Cover image: Shutterstock

Royalties from the sale of this book go to the Catholic Near East Welfare Association to assist the Church in the Holy Land.

PRINTED IN THE UNITED STATES OF AMERICA

## About the Author

George Martin is the founding editor of *God's Word Today* magazine. He has written numerous articles on Scripture as well as the books *Reading God's Word Today*, *Bringing the Gospel of Mark to Life*, *Bringing the Gospel of Matthew to Life*, *Bringing the Gospel of Luke to Life*, and *Bringing the Gospel of John to Life*, which won first place in the Scripture category in the Association of Catholic Publishers' 2017 "Excellence in Publishing Awards."

# CONTENTS

# PREFACE

The origin of this book lies in the background information provided in my expositions of the four Gospels: *Bringing the Gospel of Matthew to Life, Bringing the Gospel of Mark to Life, Bringing the Gospel of Luke to Life, and Bringing the Gospel of John to Life.* This background information helps fill in the gaps in our knowledge about the world in which Jesus grew up and carried out his ministry. To understand Jesus and his message, we need to understand as best we can the world in which he lived. The Gospels presume some familiarity with this world and often mention features of it without explaining them. What kind of town was Nazareth? Who were the Sadducees, that they would try to trip up Jesus? What did Jesus have in mind when he spoke of Gehenna, which is not mentioned in the Old Testament or explained in the New? What kind of a Messiah did Jews expect God to send, and how did Jesus live up to their expectations?

This book reformats and revises the background information found in my Gospel expositions, with many new entries added. It is meant to be user friendly rather than exhaustive. An index at the back of the book lists topics by key words, and maps help locate towns and regions.

Special acknowledgment is due Kevin Perrotta, who edited earlier versions of much of this material in the course of his editing of the Gospel volumes, and who translated the quotation from the *Psalms of Solomon.*

# Abbreviations Used for Books of the Bible

| | | | |
|---|---|---|---|
| Acts | Acts | 2 Kings | 2 Kings |
| Amos | Amos | Lamentations | Lam |
| Baruch | Baruch | Leviticus | Lev |
| 1 Chronicles | 1 Chron | Luke | Luke |
| 2 Chronicles | 2 Chron | 1 Maccabees | 1 Macc |
| Colossians | Col | 2 Maccabees | 2 Macc |
| 1 Corinthians | 1 Cor | Malachi | Mal |
| 2 Corinthians | 2 Cor | Mark | Mark |
| Daniel | Dan | Matthew | Matt |
| Deuteronomy | Deut | Micah | Micah |
| Ecclesiastes | Eccl | Nahum | Nahum |
| Ephesians | Eph | Nehemiah | Neh |
| Esther | Esther | Numbers | Num |
| Exodus | Exod | Obadiah | Obad |
| Ezekiel | Ezek | 1 Peter | 1 Pet |
| Ezra | Ezra | 2 Peter | 2 Pet |
| Galatians | Gal | Philemon | Phlm |
| Genesis | Gen | Philippians | Phil |
| Habakkuk | Hab | Proverbs | Prov |
| Haggai | Hag | Psalms | Psalm |
| Hebrews | Heb | Revelation | Rev |
| Hosea | Hosea | Romans | Rom |
| Isaiah | Isaiah | Ruth | Ruth |
| James | James | 1 Samuel | 1 Sam |
| Jeremiah | Jer | 2 Samuel | 2 Sam |
| Job | Job | Sirach | Sirach |
| Joel | Joel | Song of Songs | Song |
| John | John | 1 Thessalonians | 1 Thess |
| 1 John | 1 John | 2 Thessalonians | 2 Thess |
| 2 John | 2 John | 1 Timothy | 1 Tim |
| 3 John | 3 John | 2 Timothy | 2 Tim |
| Jonah | Jonah | Titus | Titus |
| Joshua | Joshua | Tobit | Tobit |
| Jude | Jude | Wisdom | Wisd |
| Judges | Judg | Zechariah | Zech |
| Judith | Judith | Zephaniah | Zeph |
| 1 Kings | 1 Kings | | |

# 1

# DAILY LIFE IN
# THE TIME OF JESUS

### *What is the Aramaic language?*

Aramaic was originally the language of the Arameans,
a people living in what is today Syria (Gen 25:20). Their
language was adopted by others, becoming an international diplomatic language (2 Kings 18:26) and eventually the language of the Persian Empire. Aramaic became the common language of Jews living in Palestine
while they were under Persian rule (much as Spanish
became the common language of most of South America because of its time under Spanish rule). As a result
of the conquests of Alexander the Great in the fourth
century, Greek became the common language of the
eastern Mediterranean world. Yet Aramaic persisted as
the native language of rural Galileans, and was the native language of Jesus.

### *Why were banquets so popular?*

Banquets played important social and religious roles
at the time of Jesus. They were not only a chance for

ordinary people to enjoy ample food and wine, which they otherwise rarely did, but also a form of entertainment in a world that offered few diversions compared to the modern world. Banquets marked special occasions, such as weddings (Matt 22:2; John 2:1–10) or the homecoming of a wayward son (Luke 15:23). Those who were wealthy could feast every day (Luke 16:19). Banquets were also used to celebrate religious feasts, such as Passover (Exod 12:1–28). It was the custom at Greek banquets for diners to recline on their left side on cushions or couches arranged in a U-shape. Servants served the food on low tables inside the U. Jews adopted the custom of reclining during banquets, as John shows in his account of the Last Supper (John 13:12, 23–25). The prophets spoke of God providing a banquet for his people (Isaiah 25:6), and Jesus used a feast as an image for the reign of God (Matt 8:11; 22:1–14; Luke 13:24–29; 14:15–24). Having plenty of good food to eat would have sounded heavenly to Jesus' listeners.

### What was distinctive about Jewish burial practices at the time of Jesus?

Jewish burials took place as soon as possible after death. The corpse was washed and anointed with ointments and perfumes and wrapped in cloth. Ordinary Jews were buried in simple graves dug in the ground; in the Jerusalem area, some wealthier Jews were buried in cave-like tombs carved into the limestone hillsides surrounding the city. These tombs usually contained several chambers and served entire families for several generations. Burials in family tombs were usually a two-step process. First, the corpse lay on a shelf in the tomb for about a year. Then, after the flesh had decayed away, the bones were collected and placed in a pit containing the bones of the person's ancestors. Or, in Jerusalem at the time of Jesus, bones were often placed instead in an ossuary, a lidded box carved from limestone; typically, such boxes were about twenty-four by eighteen by twelve inches. The box was then set in a recess in the tomb complex. Sometimes the bones of several members of a family were placed in the same box. In 1990, archaeologists excavating a tomb on the southern edge of Jerusalem found a bone box with an Aramaic form of the name "Caiaphas" inscribed on it. Inside were bones identified as those of a man about sixty, an adult woman, a teenage boy, a young child, and two infants. Archaeologists believe that the bones of the man are those of the Caiaphas who was high priest from A.D. 18 to 36 (see John 11:49).

## What kind of clothing did people wear?

The two basic items of clothing at the time of Jesus were the tunic and the cloak (see Luke 6:29; Acts 9:39). The tunic was an inner garment often made by folding a rectangle of cloth, sometimes linen, over on itself and stitching the sides, with openings for the head and arms. The cloak, often wool, was an outer garment, perhaps a loose-fitting robe or a rectangular cloth that one draped around oneself. These garments were worn by both men and women, with only color and decoration distinguishing them. A Jewish man's cloak would have tassels (Num 15:37–40; Deut 22:12). Belts were used to cinch tunics and cloaks. A head covering could be simply a cloth draped or tied around the head; leather sandals protected the feet. The upper class could afford imported silk and dyes, and their clothing proclaimed their status.

### Was crucifixion a fact of life?

Most everyone at the time of Jesus had heard of crucifixions even if they had not witnessed them personally. Crucifixion was an exceedingly cruel form of execution used by a number of ancient peoples. Rome adopted crucifixion as its way of executing slaves, rebels, and lower-class, violent criminals. The Romans crucified many both before and after Jesus, including thousands when Rome put down the Jewish revolt of A.D. 66–70. Crucifixions were done in a variety of ways using different styles of crosses. Common Roman practice was to first scourge the one to be crucified, to increase suffering. Then the condemned was forced to carry a crossbeam to the place of execution, where an upright post would already be in place. Roman crucifixions were done at public sites, such as along a busy road, in order to make them a public display. The one to be crucified was stripped of his clothing, and his arms were tied or nailed to the crossbeam. The crossbeam was then lifted up and fixed to the upright beam at a notch cut either in its top or in its side. Usually the person's feet were nailed or tied to the upright beam. Romans often posted a sign indicating the crime for which the person was being crucified. Despite their suffering, those who were crucified could survive for several days, tormented by pain, thirst, insects, and the shame of dying naked before others. Death usually resulted from shock or suffocation when chest muscles gave out. A body was sometimes left on the cross until it disintegrated, eaten by rats and vultures. Crucifixion was designed to be as painful and degrading a death as possible. Rome used crucifixion not merely as a punishment but also as a warning of what would happen to those who challenged Roman authority.

### *What did people eat?*

Bread was the basic food of ordinary people in Palestine at the time of Jesus and provided a substantial part of their daily calorie intake. Most families baked their own bread daily in an outdoor oven and ate bread at every meal. Bread was usually made from wheat; barley bread was cheaper but less desirable. Bread made up so much of the diet that the word for bread could be used to refer to food in general. Grain was also eaten parched ("roasted" — Ruth 2:14). Legumes such as beans and lentils, and vegetables such as cucumbers and onions rounded out meals, along with fruits such as grapes, figs, dates, and pomegranates, among others.

Grapes could be processed into wine or raisins. Olives were eaten whole or crushed for oil, which was used in cooking and dipping. Goats and sheep provided milk, often processed into yogurt and cheese. Fish from the Sea of Galilee and the Mediterranean were consumed fresh (John 21:9–10), or dried, salted, or pickled to preserve them, and were eaten whole or as a condiment for bread. Herbs, spices, and salt added taste to even simple meals. Ordinary people ate meat on special occasions, such as feasts (Luke 15:23); the extent to which meat was eaten more often is debated today. Meals were eaten with the fingers, with pieces of bread used as edible spoons to scoop up porridges and soak up sauces (Ruth 2:14; John 13:26), as is still the custom in some Middle Eastern cultures today. Members of the upper class ate much better than ordinary people: imported wines graced their tables, along with ample meat.

### How common was farming?

Farmers made up most of the population of rural Galilee. Unlike American farmers, who tend to live in isolated houses on their farms, Galilean farmers lived together in small towns and villages and went out to work their fields. They grew grain crops, including wheat and barley; fruits, such as grapes, olives, and figs; and vegetables, such as lentils, beans, peas, and cucumbers. Galilee contained some prime farmland in its valleys, including the broad valleys north and south of Nazareth. Much of the prime land had been expropriated by rulers, such as Herod Antipas at the time of Jesus, who either had it managed for them or entrusted it to their influential supporters. Some farmers worked as tenant farmers or day laborers on these estates. Most farmers owned their own plots of land, which were often small and were sometimes on a rocky hillside that had to be terraced to support crops. Farmers were subject to tithes and taxes on their crops, which by some estimates added up to 40 percent of their harvests. These farmers were better off than day laborers, but a few bad harvests could lead to indebtedness and loss of land.

### How was fishing done on the Sea of Galilee?

In the first century, the Sea of Galilee was ringed with towns with harbors and was commercially fished, as it has been up to the present day. Commercial fishing, rather than sport fishing, is reflected in the Gospels. There were about eighteen species of fish in the Sea of Galilee, with three categories making up the bulk of commercial catches: sardines, carp, and tilapia. Tilapia feed on plankton and must be caught with nets, not with hooks and bait. Tilapia weigh up to four pounds and swim in schools around the northern end of the Sea of Galilee during wintertime; the great nettings of fish reported in the Gospels were likely catches of tilapia. Fishermen used various forms of nets, including circular nets that were cast by hand and dragnets that were deployed from boats. Remains of a first-century fishing boat were discovered in 1986 buried in the mud near the shore of the Sea of Galilee at Ginnosar (ancient Gennesaret), an area Jesus visited (Matt 14:34; Mark 6:53). This boat, twenty-six and a half feet long, seven and a half feet wide, and four and a half feet deep, was apparently typical of the fishing boats mentioned in the Gospels. It had a rounded stern and may have had decks fore and aft. It would have had a small square sail and a crew of four rowers and a rudder man. It could have carried an additional ten to twelve passengers when it was not transporting nets and fish.

### How had Greek language and culture made inroads in Palestine?

Alexander the Great (ruled 336–323 B.C.) of Macedonia (northern Greece) conquered the eastern Mediterranean world. Thereafter, the Greek language became the common international language and the everyday language of many of the lands he conquered. Many Jews living outside Palestine adopted Greek; Jews living in Egypt translated the Hebrew Scriptures into Greek in the third and second centuries B.C. The New Testament was written in Greek as the most commonly understood language. Even Paul's letter to Rome was written in Greek, not Latin. The early Church, being overwhelmingly Greek-speaking, used the Greek translation of the Old Testament as its Scripture. Greek culture, including philosophy, architectural styles, and enjoyment of the theater, had Jewish adherents in some of the larger cities of Palestine, including Jerusalem, but does not seem to have penetrated the small villages and rural areas of Galilee.

## What is the Hebrew language?

Hebrew was the vernacular language of the Israelite people until after the exile; most of the Old Testament was written in Hebrew. After the exile Aramaic, a related language, became the most common spoken language of Jews living in Palestine, and small portions of a couple of books of the Old Testament are in Aramaic. At the time of Jesus, many Jews could not read or understand Hebrew, and Aramaic translations of the Scriptures were sometimes used in synagogues in Palestine. The Gospel of John uses the word "Hebrew" to refer to the Aramaic as well as the Hebrew language.

## Why was hospitality so valued?

The practice of welcoming guests, including strangers, into one's home for meals and lodging is common in the Old and New Testaments. Abraham provides an example of generous hospitality when he begs three traveling strangers to accept a snack from him but then serves them a banquet (Gen 18:1–8). Abraham's nephew Lot pleads with passing strangers to spend the night in his house rather than sleep in the town square (Gen 19:1–3). Job lists hospitality among his upright deeds: "No stranger lodged in the street, / but I opened my door to wayfarers" (Job 31:32). Those who traveled usually had to rely on the hospitality of others. Caravan inns on main routes provided shelter for travelers and animals (Luke 10:34–35), but there were no inns in ordinary towns and villages. Jesus depended on the hospitality of his followers, including Peter (Mark 1:29–34; 2:1) and Martha and Mary (Luke 10:38–42). Jesus included hospitality among his concerns on judgment day: "I was … a stranger and you welcomed me" (Matt 25:35). The practice of hospitality is evident in Acts (Acts 10:21–23; 16:15; 28:7), and the letters of the New Testament hold hospitality in high regard (Rom 12:13; 1 Tim 3:2; 5:10; Titus 1:8; Heb 13:2).

### What were houses like?

First-century Palestinian houses ranged from the very small to the truly sumptuous. Ordinary people often lived in one-room houses that usually shared an open courtyard with other one-room houses. Much of life was lived outdoors; cooking was done in the courtyard. Rooms were dark and sometimes windowless and used for sleeping and shelter from the elements. In eastern Galilee (in Capernaum, for example), houses were built of basalt, a dark volcanic stone common in the area. Floors were made of basalt cobblestones; roofs were made of beams overlaid with thatch and clay. In Jericho, a city in the lower Jordan River valley, mud brick was used for the walls of ordinary dwellings. The wealthy elite lived in fine houses with mosaic floors, frescoed (painted plaster) walls, and elegant columns. The remains of several mansions belonging to the wealthy have been excavated in Jerusalem. One of these houses had several stories and more than six thousand square feet under its roof; it probably belonged to a member of a high-priestly family.

### Can we throw light on oil lamps?

During much of the Old Testament era, an Israelite oil lamp was a very simple affair, a shallow pottery bowl that had edges turned up to form a channel for a wick. Lamps burned olive oil; wicks were commonly made of flax, which could be grown locally (cotton was imported). Oil lamp design changed late in the Old Testament era, with tops added to minimize spilling. At the time of Jesus, the common single wick oil lamp was rather small and would fit into the palm of one's hand. It gave off roughly one candle power of light — feeble by modern standards but a welcome light in the darkness of homes with few if any windows (see Luke 15:8). What are called lamps in the parable of the wise and foolish virgins (Matt 25:1–13) were likely torches made of rags wound around sticks and soaked in olive oil, more suitable than oil lamps to light a parade at night.

### Was leprosy in biblical times the same disease as leprosy today?

In the Old and New Testaments, the Hebrew and Greek words translated "leprosy" refer to a variety of skin conditions and infections. In the New Testament period, one of these conditions may have been what is called leprosy today (Hansen's disease). Some of these skin conditions went away in time; some did not. A skin condition that resulted in a certain kind of abnormal appearance made the afflicted person ritually impure, or unclean. Old Testament regulations specified that priests were to determine whether a skin condition was "leprosy"; if it was, the person with the skin disease was excluded from the community as unclean (Lev 13). Priests likewise judged whether a person's leprosy had gone away, in which case the person underwent purification rituals before rejoining the community (Lev 14). These procedures indicate that what was at stake was ritual purity. Exclusion of the afflicted person from the community prevented the spread of ritual uncleanness; there was little understanding of the nature of diseases or of how they were spread.

## What were Jewish marriage practices at the time of Jesus?

The love of wife and husband for each other could be just as heartfelt in ancient as in modern times, and sexual attraction just as passionate (see the Song of Songs). Yet the understanding and practice of marriage in the Old Testament has its differences from marriage in the modern Western world. The primary purpose of marriage was to beget children, specifically sons who could continue the father's family name and inherit the father's family lands. Hence shame befell a barren wife, however much her husband might love her (1 Sam

1:1–8), since infertility was always attributed to the woman, never to the man. If a husband died without leaving a son, his brother was to marry his widow and beget an heir for him (Deut 25:5–6). A man could have more than one wife (Deut 21:15–17), but a wife could not have more than one husband, for that would create family heritage tangles. Inheritance passed to sons, with a double share to the oldest (Deut 21:17). Only by exception could daughters inherit (Num 27:8), and then with restrictions to keep the inheritance within the father's clan (Num 36:6–9). Marriages were arrangements between families as well as between husband and wife. Particularly when those getting married were young — possibly as early as puberty for a girl but a few years older for a boy — their fathers arranged their betrothal, sometimes drawing up a contract (see Tobit 7:13). A betrothed woman might continue to live with her family for a period of time (Matt 1:18). There was no wedding ceremony as such, but a party to celebrate the wife moving into the home of her husband (Matt 22:2–10; 25:1–13; Mark 2:19; John 2:1–10).

### *What role did patrons play?*

There was a great disparity in the ancient Mediterranean world between the few who were wealthy and powerful and the many who were poor and powerless. A patron was a person of wealth and influence to whom a person of lesser status turned for help. Patrons provided financial assistance or used their influence to benefit their clients. Doing favors brought honor and prestige for patrons and the loyalty and praise of their clients. Wealthy people often functioned as patrons of their city by paying for public buildings or projects; today we call someone who endows a concert hall a "patron of the arts." An ancient inscription found in Corinth speaks of an Erastus who paid out of his own funds for the paving of a street; this is likely the same Erastus who was a Christian and city treasurer (Rom 16:23). The centurion who "built the synagogue" (Luke 7:2) for the people of Capernaum acted as a patron. Women as well as men could be patrons. Mary Magdalene, Joanna, the wife of Herod's steward Chuza, and Susanna "provided for" Jesus and his disciples "out of their resources" (Luke 8:2–3); Joanna at least would have had significant resources at her disposal. Paul converted a woman named Lydia in Philippi (Acts 16:14–15). As a dealer in expensive purple cloth she was wealthy and in charge of a household. Lydia acted as Paul's patron, having him stay in her home and supporting him, and making her house available as a place where the Church could meet (Acts 16:40).

## Who were the poor and the rich?

In first-century Galilee, few were well enough off to be what we would consider middle class and very few were wealthy. Most supported themselves by farming, usually on small plots of land. They were able to raise enough to pay taxes and feed their families, but barely.

Bad harvests could mean going into debt, losing one's land, and becoming a day laborer. Herod Antipas controlled the prime farmland, entrusting some of it to his key supporters. The minority who did not farm commonly worked as craftsmen (carpenters, potters, tanners), merchants, fishermen, servants, shepherds, or tax collectors. Some Jews were slaves, although slavery was not as common as in other parts of the Roman Empire. Most Galileans could be thought of as the working poor. At the bottom of the working poor were day laborers, dependent on being hired each day. Worst off were those unable to work: the blind, crippled, leprous. Unless they had relatives to support them, the nonworking poor survived by begging. Jesus' followers mirrored the composition of Galilean society: most were working poor, very few were wealthy. Jesus' ministry was marked by concern for the nonworking poor: "the blind regain their sight, the lame walk, lepers are cleansed, the deaf hear, the dead are raised, the poor have the good news proclaimed to them" (Luke 7:22). Being wealthy posed the danger of using one's wealth only for oneself (Luke 12:16–21; 16:19–31). Wealth was properly used to help those who could not provide for themselves (Luke 12:33; 14:12–14; 18:22; 19:8).

### How did servants and slaves differ?

Both servants and slaves did the bidding of others, and may even have done identical work, but with a major difference: servants were hired, slaves were owned. A servant was free to decide whom to work for and could quit; a slave had no choice but to work for his or her owner. At the time of Jesus, one became a slave by being born to a woman slave, by being taken as a prisoner of war, by incurring a debt one could not pay off, by voluntarily becoming a slave to avoid starvation, or by being kidnapped. Slaves made up around a fifth of the population in the Roman Empire. Many owners treated their slaves badly; some owners were cruel and sexually abusive. Yet there are important differences as well as similarities between slavery in the first-century Roman Empire and slavery in the Americas in the seventeenth to nineteenth centuries, and further differences as well as similarities between slavery in Palestine and slavery in other parts of the Roman Empire. In the world of Jesus, slavery was not based on race: the slaves referred to in Jesus' parables are usually Jews owned by other Jews. Slaves could own property (including other slaves!) and hold important positions; a few slaves were better educated than their owners. Some slaves served as managers, doctors, and bankers, although most slaves in Palestine were farm workers or domestic servants. A few freely chose slavery because it offered them guaranteed employment, preferring it over working as day laborers. Most slaves, however, wanted to be free. Slaves could be freed after a certain period of service; a slave of a Roman citizen was generally given citizenship upon being freed. There are different Greek words for servant and slave, but in the Gospels the *New*

*American Bible* usually translates the Greek word for slave as "servant" (e.g., Luke 2:29; 12:37; 14:17; 15:22; 19:13; 20:10; 22:50), apparently to avoid confusing the ancient practice of slavery with slavery in the American experience.

## What was a talent worth?

A talent was originally a measure of weight. In its origin it may have been the weight a load-bearer could be expected to carry, somewhere between fifty and seventy-five pounds. In the book of Revelation, the "large hailstones like huge weights" that fell onto people are literally hailstones "weighing a talent" (Rev 16:21). A talent came to designate a weight of precious metal, of gold (Exod 38:24) or silver (Exod 38:25). At the time of Jesus, a talent was the largest monetary unit, equivalent to six thousand denarii, where a denarius was the usual daily wage for an ordinary worker. In the *New American Bible* translation of Jesus' parable of the two debtors (Matt 18:23–35), the "huge amount" that the first debtor owes is literally "tens of thousands of talents." Since ten thousand was the largest number used in counting and a talent the largest monetary unit, the first debtor owed the largest amount that could be conceived.

## Why were tax collectors so despised?

Those who collected taxes were almost universally scorned by Jews in Palestine at the time of Jesus and were spoken of in the same breath with sinners (Matt 11:19). They were despised for several reasons. First, the tax system lent itself to abuse. One arrangement was to auction off the right to collect taxes to the highest bidder and then allow the tax collector to keep anything he could collect over that amount. That was a license for greed and extortion, and many tax collectors took advantage of it. Second, there were many forms of taxation, and together they extracted a sizeable portion of the income of ordinary people — up to 40 percent, by some estimates. Third, Jewish tax collectors were agents, directly or indirectly, of Rome. After about a century of Jewish self-rule, Rome had taken away Jewish independence in 63 B.C. and had imposed tribute or taxes. As a result of these factors, tax collectors were considered unscrupulous extortionists and were despised for working on behalf of a foreign power and draining people's livelihoods.

**2**

# THE LAY OF THE LAND
## *Regions and Places*

### *What was the Decapolis?*

The Greek word *decapolis* means "ten cities," and it originally referred to a confederation of ten cities chiefly situated east of the Jordan River. At the time of Jesus the Decapolis was an administrative district attached to the Roman province of Syria. The cities of the Decapolis had a predominantly or entirely Gentile population, were Greek in their culture and religion, and were wealthy compared with the Jewish villages of Galilee. Archaeologists have uncovered colonnaded, paved streets, as well as theaters, temples, sports facilities, and other evidence of Greek lifestyle in cities of the Decapolis.

### *What kind of desert is there in Palestine?*

The "desert of Judea" (Matt 3:1) is a rocky wilderness, not a desert of fine blowing sand. It is a barren region because it receives little rain. The Judean desert stretches from the Mount of Olives and the eastern outskirts of Jerusalem down to the Jordan River and Dead Sea, far below sea level. Although in its lower elevations it is devoid of plant life, sufficient scrubby vegetation grows in its upper elevations to pasture the goats and sheep of nomadic shepherds.

### What was Galilee like, the native area of "Jesus the Galilean" (Matt 26:69)?

Galilee was the northern region of ancient Palestine. Most of the Galilean sites mentioned in the Gospels were in what was considered lower Galilee in the time of Jesus: a roughly circular area twenty to twenty-five miles across, with the Sea of Galilee on the east and the coastal hills of the Mediterranean on the west. Nazareth was near the southern edge of lower Galilee, and Capernaum was in the northeast. The general character of Galilee was rural. The two most significant cities in lower Galilee — Sepphoris and Tiberias — seem to have had little cultural impact on those who did not live within them. Most of the inhabitants of Galilee supported themselves by farming or fishing and lived in villages or small towns. Galilee contained the estates of its ruler, Herod Antipas, and his wealthy supporters, and some Galileans worked as tenant farmers or day laborers on these estates. There was not much of a middle class in Galilee; there was a small, wealthy elite and many ordinary and rather poor people. The Galilee to which Jesus addressed himself was primarily the

Galilee of ordinary people: while his message reached members of the upper class, the Gospels never describe him going into Sepphoris or Tiberias, even though Sepphoris lay only four miles from Nazareth, and Tiberias seven miles from Capernaum. Galilee during the ministry of Jesus has sometimes been described as a paganized area, a region of lax religious observance, and a hotbed of revolutionary nationalism, but none of these characterizations is accurate. In general, Galilee was Jewish rather than pagan, and the Jews of rural Galilee were traditional in their religious practices, relatively uninfluenced by Greek culture, and slow to heed calls to revolt.

## What was Gennesaret, where Jesus healed many people?

Gennesaret (1 Macc 11:67; Matt 14:34; Mark 6:53) is a plain on the northwest shore of the Sea of Galilee, lying between Capernaum and Magdala. According to Josephus, a first-century Jewish historian, Gennesaret extends three and one half miles along the shore of the Sea of Galilee and two and one half miles inland. Josephus describes it as "wonderful in its characteristics and its beauty" and praises its fertility: "thanks to its rich soil, there is not a plant that does not flourish there, and the inhabitants grow everything. The air is so temperate that it suits the most diverse species … it is watered by a spring with great fertilizing power, known locally as Capernaum" (*Jewish War*, III, 10:8).

### What is the significance of the location of Gethsemane?

After Jesus' last supper with his disciples, he went with them "to a place called Gethsemane" (Matt 26:36; Mark 14:32), which was on the Mount of Olives (Matt 26:30; Luke 22:39) "across the Kidron valley" (John 18:1) from Jerusalem. Jesus had previously made use of the site to meet with his disciples (Luke 22:39; John 18:2). A tradition dating back to the fourth century locates Gethsemane on the western slope of the Mount of Olives, directly across the Kidron Valley from Jerusalem. Olive trees have been grown on the Mount of Olives from ancient until modern times, giving it its name. "Gethsemane" is derived from the Hebrew and Aramaic words for "olive press," and there is evidence of an ancient olive press near the traditional site of Gethsemane. The Gospel of John describes it as a garden (John 18:1) but does not call it Gethsemane; Matthew and Mark call it Gethsemane but do not characterize it as a garden. To refer to it as "the Garden of Gethsemane" synthesizes what the Gospels tell us. More significant than its name is its location. Those who came at night to arrest Jesus carrying lanterns and torches (John 18:3) would have been visible to him as soon as they left Jerusalem. Jesus could easily have ascended the Mount of Olives and escaped before they reached Gethsemane. A twenty minute walk would have taken him into the beginning of the Judean wilderness, where it would have been impossible for anyone to find him at night. Jesus' agony in the garden was also his waiting in the garden for Judas to arrive, in acceptance of his Father's will for him.

### Why was Golgotha called "the place of the skull" (Luke 23:33)?

During the Old Testament era, the limestone hillside west of Jerusalem was quarried for building blocks. Seams of quality limestone were dug out; poor stone was left unquarried. Eventually the good stone played out, and the quarry was abandoned. At the time of Jesus, the old quarry lay just outside the western wall of Jerusalem near a city gate. A hump of unquarried rock jutted up perhaps twenty to thirty feet. Romans used this mound of rock as a place to crucify criminals, since it made a public display of their deaths. The site was called Golgotha, from the Aramaic word for skull, likely because the unquarried hump of rock was shaped like the top of a skull (Luke refers to the site as "the place called the Skull" — Luke 23:33). The Latin word for skull gives us the name "Calvary." Today the site of Golgotha is within the Church of the Holy Sepulchre in Jerusalem.

### Where was Idumea?

The southern portion of Palestine was the land of the tribe of Judah and part of the kingdom of David and Solomon. After Babylon conquered Jerusalem in 587 B.C.,

Jewish control of this area was lost. Edomites, whose traditional homeland, Edom, lay southeast of the Dead Sea, migrated westward under pressure from an Arab tribe known as the Nabateans. Displaced Edomites settled in the southern part of Palestine, and the region then became known as Idumea (Mark 3:8). The Maccabean Jewish ruler John Hyrcanus I conquered Idumea in 129 B.C. and forcibly converted the Idumeans to Judaism. Herod the Great's father was Idumean, and his mother was Nabatean, making his Jewish identity suspect in the eyes of many. At the time of Jesus' public ministry, Idumea was part of the area governed by Pontius Pilate. Idumea is mentioned five times in 1 and 2 Maccabees, but only in Mark 3:8 in the New Testament.

### *Where is Jacob's Well?*

Abraham's grandson Jacob bought a plot of land near Shechem (Gen 33:18–19), about thirty miles north of Jerusalem. In New Testament times, the remains of Shechem lay in Samaria; today they are adjacent to Nablus, a Palestinian town on the West Bank. John's Gospel recounts that "Jacob's well" was on this plot of land (John 4:5–6). The Old Testament does not mention Jacob's well, but if the plot of land that Jacob bought had value for raising crops or cattle, it likely had a source of water. Today there is a well traditionally identified as Jacob's well several hundred feet from the ruins of Shechem. This well is about seventy-five feet deep, a man-made shaft reaching down to a water source.

### *Where does the Jordan River flow from and to?*

The sources of the Jordan River lie in the foothills of Mount Hermon; one of these sources is a powerful spring at Caesarea Philippi. From these foothills the river runs south, emptying into the north end of the Sea of Galilee and emerging from its south end. At the time of Jesus, the upper stretch of the Jordan River formed the boundary between the territory ruled by Herod Agrippa and the territory to the east ruled by his half-brother Philip. From the Sea of Galilee the Jordan River runs south until it empties into the Dead Sea, which has no outlet. It is about sixty-five miles in a straight line from the Sea of Galilee to the Dead Sea, but the Jordan River meanders for one hundred thirty-five miles as it flows between these two bodies of water. The traditional site for "Bethany across the Jordan" where John the Baptist baptized (John 1:28) lies on a stream that flows into the Jordan River about five miles north of the Dead Sea.

### *What is Judea and what is it connection with Jews?*

Judea was the region of Palestine around and to the south of Jerusalem. It was originally the territory of the tribe of Judah, which gave it its name. Israelites from this region who had been in exile in Babylon returned to Judea after 538 B.C. Thereafter they began to be called Judeans, which passed through Greek and Latin and came into English as the word "Jews."

## What is the Kidron Valley?

Jerusalem is separated on its east from the Mount of Olives by the Kidron Valley. This valley is mentioned by name only once in the New Testament: "Jesus went out with his disciples across the Kidron valley to where there was a garden" (John 18:1). The word in John's Gospel that is translated as "valley" is, literally, "winter-flowing," for the Kidron is a dry ravine that becomes a brook during the winter rainy season. Hence in the ten times that the Kidron is mentioned in the Old Testament, the *New American Bible* calls it the "Wadi Kidron" (see 2 Sam 15:23), with "wadi" being an Arabic word for a valley or ravine that is dry except during the rainy season.

## Is the Mount of Olives a mountain?

Not by Rocky Mountain standards. The Mount of Olives is a north-south ridge of limestone hills lying just east of Jerusalem. The tallest of these hills has an elevation of about 2,700 feet and rises several hundred feet above the hills of Jerusalem. The Kidron Valley lies between Jerusalem and the Mount of Olives on its western side; the villages of Bethany and Bethphage lay on its eastern slopes. The Judean desert (Mark 1:12; Luke 1:80) begins at the eastern foot of the Mount of Olives (see 2 Sam 15:23).

## Do we know on which mountain Jesus was transfigured?

The Gospels of Matthew and Mark tell of Jesus taking Peter, James, and John "up a high mountain" (Matt 17:1; Mark 9:2). Jesus and his disciples had been in the region of Caesarea Philippi (Matt 16:13; see Mark 8:27), which was on the southernmost slope of Mount Hermon, the highest peak in the area. Mount Hermon lies on the border between present-day Lebanon and Syria; it has an elevation of 9,232 feet and is covered with snow for most of the year. Since the Gospels do not name the mountain on which Jesus was transfigured, we cannot be sure of its location. Mount Hermon certainly qualifies as a "high mountain." On the other hand, some days passed between Jesus' traveling to Caesarea Philippi and his ascending a mountain (Matt 17:1; Mark 9:2), allowing time for him to have gone to another region. Uncertainty over the site of the transfiguration led to speculation about various locations. Eusebius (a bishop, Church historian, and geographer who died around A.D. 340) thought it was either Mount Hermon or Mount Tabor in Galilee. In A.D. 348, Bishop Cyril of Jerusalem advocated Tabor, and St. Jerome subsequently supported his choice. Tabor is a majestic rounded hill rising 1,485 feet above the Jezreel Valley. There was apparently a village on Tabor's summit at the time of Jesus, making it a less-private location than Mount Hermon. Cyril and Jerome might have had pilgrims in mind when they proposed Tabor, for it lay only six miles from Nazareth and was far more convenient for pilgrims to visit than the rugged heights of Hermon.

### Have they found Peter's House in Capernaum, where Jesus stayed?

In Capernaum, archaeologists have found the remains of an ancient neighborhood of houses clustered around courtyards. An octagonal church was erected over and in place of one of the houses in the fifth century; octagonal or circular churches were built to mark holy places. Beneath the center of the church are the remains of a small one- or two-room building that was constructed around 65 B.C. Its walls and floor were made of unworked basalt stones — the local black, volcanic rock — and would have supported a roof of beams and tree branches covered with thatch and earth. The interior of this building measured about twenty by twenty feet, and it shared a courtyard with other similar small buildings. Archaeologists have found fishhooks and broken kitchenware indicating that it was used as a family home at the time of Jesus. Later in the first century this room was set aside for special use. Its walls and floor were plastered (unlike other houses in Capernaum), and Christians began carving prayers in the plaster, which suggests that it was a venerated site used for Christian gatherings. An arch was added in the fourth century to support a tile roof. Egeria, a European nun who came on pilgrimage to the Holy Land sometime around A.D. 390, wrote in her travel notes, "In Capernaum a house church was made out of the house of Peter, and its walls still stand today." Egeria's words and the archaeological evidence make it very probable that the venerated room was the "house of Peter" (Matt 8:14). Subsequently the octagonal church was built over the site. This church was destroyed in the seventh century, perhaps during a Persian invasion. Capernaum went into a steady decline after an eighth-century earthquake and was abandoned in the eleventh century. A modern church was dedicated in 1992, with a glass floor that allows worshippers to gaze down on the remains of Peter's house — the house in which Jesus stayed and used as the base of his public ministry in Galilee (see Mark 1:29–34; 2:1–12; 3:20).

### How can the Pool of Bethesda have "five porticoes" (John 5:2)?

A short valley slopes down from the north toward the site of the Temple in Jerusalem. In the eighth century B.C., a dam was built across the valley to capture rain runoff, forming what is referred to in the Old Testament as "the upper pool" (2 Kings 18:17; Isaiah 7:3). Initially a channel fed water from this reservoir to the Temple. A second large pool was built south of the dam by the high priest Simon around 200 B.C. (see Sirach 50:3). The pools were configured roughly like a figure 8 with trapezoidal sides (see the map of Jerusalem on page 135). The southern pool was roughly 160 by 200 feet and the northern pool roughly 130 by 170 feet — together the area of an American football field. By the time of Jesus, the pools were no longer simply reservoirs. Porticoes (covered colonnades) had been built along the sides of the pools and on the twenty-foot wide dam that separated them. John's Gospel refers to the site as "a pool called in Hebrew Bethesda, with five porticoes" (John 5:2). The southern pool has steps and broad landings leading down into it, an indication that this pool was used for bodily immersion and ritual purification. The recently excavated Pool of Siloam is of similar design and was also a huge outdoor ritual bath (*miqveh* in Hebrew). The northern pool of Bethesda fed water as needed to the southern pool through a conduit that could be opened and closed; this satisfied the requirement that a ritual bath be fed by flowing water. The pools eventually became buried beneath rubble. They were discovered by archaeologists in modern times, helping readers of John's Gospel visualize what a pool with five porticoes looked like.

### What was the Pool of Siloam?

Biblical Jerusalem had but a single spring as a source of water. During the period of the Israelite kings, the spring was located outside the eastern wall of the city in the Kidron Valley, making it vulnerable in time of war: a besieging army could seize the spring and wait until Jerusalem's cisterns ran dry. In anticipation of an

Assyrian invasion in 701 B.C. (2 Kings 18:13), King Hezekiah strengthened the walls of Jerusalem, dug a reservoir within the city, and had a roughly 1,750 foot tunnel carved through bedrock to bring water from the spring to the reservoir (2 Kings 20:20; Sirach 48:17). Then he had the spring covered over (see 2 Chron 32:30), hiding it from the Assyrian army. Other pools fed by Hezekiah's water tunnel were eventually dug in the same area. One of them was the Pool of Siloam (John 9:7), which was discovered by archaeologists in 2004. Although not completely excavated, it dates to the time of Jesus and appears to measure roughly 225 feet on a side, with paved steps and broad landings leading down into it along the lengths of its sides. Such steps and landings would be unnecessary if it were merely a water reservoir, and they indicate that it was a ritual bath (*miqveh* in Hebrew) used for bodily immersion and purification before entering the Temple. The Pool of Siloam was continuously fed by water from Hezekiah's tunnel; ritual baths required at least intermittently flowing water. Smaller indoor ritual baths found near the Temple would have provided greater privacy, but would have been inadequate to serve the tens of thousands who came to Jerusalem during pilgrimage feasts. It was the practice of one Jewish group, the Essenes, for men to wear loin cloths when using communal ritual baths; Essene women wore dresses. This may have been the practice as well of other Jews to preserve modesty when using public ritual baths like the Pool of Siloam and the Pool of Bethesda.

### Did Jesus live in the Roman Empire?

At the time of Jesus, the Roman Empire included all the lands bordering the Mediterranean Sea and extended through western Europe as far as Britain. The Roman general Pompey had intervened in a Jewish civil war in 63 B.C., conquering Jerusalem and pushing aside the ruling Jewish Hasmonean dynasty, thus bringing Palestine under Roman domination. This was a time of transition within the Roman government, as power became consolidated in an emperor and conquered lands gradually came under direct Roman rule. In this transitional period, Rome sometimes ruled through client kings, such as Herod the Great and his sons in Palestine. The Roman government was content to have the Herods rule on its behalf as long as they did so competently, were loyal to Rome, and paid taxes. Other regions were ruled as Roman provinces by governors sent from Rome. Judea became a Roman province in A.D. 6 after Rome deposed Herod's son Archelaus for incompetence. During Jesus' public ministry, Pontius Pilate was the Roman governor of Judea and some adjacent areas. In A.D. 66, many Jews in Palestine rebelled against Roman rule, with disastrous consequences. Rome put down the revolt, destroying Jerusalem in A.D. 70.

## What was Samaria and who are the Samaritans?

A region called Samaria lay north of Judea and south of Galilee, separating these two predominantly Jewish regions. In Old Testament times the area that would become known as Samaria was part of the northern kingdom of Israel after its split from the southern kingdom of Judah. The split between the kingdoms was religious as well as political: the northern kingdom established shrines as rivals to the Temple in Jerusalem. The northern kingdom was conquered by Assyria around 721 B.C.; some of its inhabitants were deported, and foreigners settled in their place (see 2 Kings 17). The Samaritans of New Testament times were considered by the Jews of Judea and Galilee to be the descendants of the foreigners and Israelites left by the Assyrians, mixed in race and religion and ritually unclean. Sirach, writing around 180 B.C., expressed scorn for Samaritans, saying that he loathed them with his whole being (Sirach 50:25–26); calling a Jew a Samaritan was an insult (John 8:48). Samaritans, on the other hand, thought of themselves as true Israelites, descendants of the tribes of Ephraim and Manasseh, who rigorously followed the law set down in the five books of Moses (Genesis through Deuteronomy). They erected a temple to God in the heart of Samaria on Mount Gerizim, the place they believed God wanted to be worshipped (see John 4:20). A Jewish ruler invaded and tore down the Samaritan temple in 128 B.C., increasing tensions

between Samaritans and Jews. Samaritans have survived as an identifiable group through the centuries,
with about seven hundred alive today. Half live in a village on a slope of Mount Gerizim and the other half in
a town near Tel Aviv.

### How large is the Sea of Galilee?

Luke aptly refers to the Sea of Galilee as a lake (Luke
5:1; 8:22–23), for it is a freshwater body thirteen miles
long and eight miles wide at most, with a maximum
depth of one hundred forty feet. The Jordan River empties into the northern end of the lake and flows out
from its southern end. In the time of Jesus the lake was
ringed with fishing villages, and it has been commercially fished into the present. The Sea of Galilee lies six
hundred ninety feet below sea level and is bordered by
high hills that are cut by steep valleys. Strong winds
can blow through these valleys and down onto the lake
and stir up sudden storms. The Sea of Galilee is also
called the Sea of Chinnereth (or Kinneret) in the Old
Testament (Num 34:11; Joshua 12:3; 13:27), the Sea of
Tiberias by John (John 6:1; 21:1) and the Lake of Gennesaret by Luke (Luke 5:1).

### What do we know about the tomb of Jesus?

At the time of Jesus, an abandoned limestone quarry
lay just outside the western wall of Jerusalem. Here
Golgotha rose as a hump of unquarried rock. Tombs
were dug in the old quarry, just as tombs were dug into

virtually all the hills surrounding biblical Jerusalem. The tomb in which Jesus' corpse was buried, located less than two hundred feet from Golgotha, was cut into the side of the quarry. This tomb had at least two chambers: a small antechamber at its entrance and a second chamber with a shelf cut into its wall where a corpse could be laid. There were likely other chambers for other corpses or for their bones after the flesh had decayed away. After Jesus' body was taken down from the cross, it was placed on the shelf in the second chamber. In the fourth century, the Roman emperor Constantine ordered a church to be built at the site of Golgotha and the tomb of Jesus. Workers cut away the hillside surrounding the tomb of Jesus in order to isolate it as a freestanding chapel. This chapel was largely destroyed in the eleventh century and has been rebuilt several times since. Today Golgotha and the tomb of Jesus are within the Church of the Holy Sepulchre in Jerusalem.

### When the Gospels speak of the world, do they always mean our universe?

In the New Testament, the Greek word *kosmos,* which is translated as "world" in the *New American Bible,* has various shades of meaning. It can refer to the created universe (Matt 25:34; Acts 17:24), or to the earth (Mark 16:15), especially as it is inhabited by humans (Matt 4:8), or to the humans inhabiting the earth (Rom 3:6, 19). It has these and additional shades of meaning in the Gospel of John, which uses "world" seventy-eight times, by far the most by any book of the New Testament. In this Gospel, "world" can stand for the earthly realm in contrast to the celestial realm or heaven (John 6:33, 51; 8:23; 13:1; 16:28). "World" can refer to humanity as it is alienated from God (John 1:29; 7:7; 12:31; 14:17; 15:18–19; 17:14). The particular shades of meaning of "world" must be determined for each passage of John's Gospel in which it occurs.

### What was Zion?

The name "Zion" has multiple associations in the Old Testament. It was originally a name for Jerusalem when it was a Jebusite stronghold; David captured "the fortress of Zion" and made it "the City of David" (2 Sam 5:7). After Solomon built his Temple north of the City of David, Zion became a name for the hill on which the Temple stood; Psalm 74:2 asks God to remember "Mount Zion where you dwell" (see also Isaiah 8:18). Zion also came to mean the city of Jerusalem (Isaiah 40:9) and its inhabitants (Isaiah 51:16). "Daughter Zion" is a poetic expression for the city of Jerusalem (Psalm 9:15) and those who live in it (Micah 4:10). There are scattered references in the New Testament to Zion, Mount Zion, and Daughter Zion.

# 3

# THE LAY OF THE LAND
## *Towns*

### *Where was Bethany?*

Bethany was a village on a southeastern slope of the Mount of Olives, about two miles from Jerusalem (John 11:18). During major feasts Jerusalem was crowded with pilgrims and accommodations were scarce; hence Jesus spent his nights in Bethany when he came to Jerusalem for Passover (Matt 21:17; Mark 11:11–12; see also Luke 21:37), although these Gospels do not make it clear whether Jesus stayed with friends or camped out. The Gospel of John presents Mary, Martha, and Lazarus as residents of Bethany (John 11:1). Luke seems to situate Mary and Martha in a village near Galilee (Luke 10:38–42); Matthew and Mark do not mention the two sisters or Lazarus. Matthew and Mark describe Jesus eating at the home of Simon the Leper in Bethany (Matt 26:6–13; Mark 14:3–9); John describes a similar meal in Bethany with Martha, Mary, and Lazarus (John 12:1–8).

## Was Bethany across the Jordan the same as Bethany?

The Gospel of John recounts that Jesus came to John the Baptist when he was baptizing at a place called Bethany across the Jordan — that is, across or on the eastern side of the Jordan River (John 1:28–29; see also John 10:40). Bethany across the Jordan thus should not be confused with the Bethany that lies two miles east of Jerusalem. Christian tradition located Bethany across the Jordan at what is now called Wadi al-Kharrar, a spring-fed tributary of the Jordan River in the modern country of Jordan. It lies about five miles north of the Dead Sea. Archaeologists have found numerous remains of ancient churches and baptismal pools at the site, and it is visited by Christian pilgrims today.

## What was the significance of Jesus being born in Bethlehem?

Bethlehem lies about five miles south of Jerusalem. Its name has been popularly interpreted to mean "house of bread;" grain crops were grown in adjacent fields (see Ruth 1:22–2:23). King David's family lived in Bethlehem (1 Sam 16:1–13), giving it its chief claim to fame in the Old Testament. It was otherwise not an impressive village. The prophet Micah called it "least among the clans of Judah" but nonetheless prophesied that "from you shall come forth for me / one who is to be ruler in Israel" (Micah 5:1). Micah's prophecy was the basis for an expectation that the Messiah would not only be a descendant of David but would also come from Bethlehem (Matt 2:4–6; John 7:42). However, this expectation of a Bethlehem origin was not shared by all at the time of Jesus (see John 7:27). Bethlehem was likely still a rather modest village at the time of Jesus' birth.

### Where was Bethphage?

Bethphage was a village on the Mount of Olives. It apparently lay somewhere west of Bethany but its exact location is unknown today. A road from Jericho to Jerusalem ran along or through Bethany and Bethphage at it made its way over the Mount of Olives on its way to Jerusalem (see Matt 21:1; Mark 11:1; Luke 19:29).

### Has the site of Bethsaida been found?

Remains of what archaeologists believe was Bethsaida were found four miles northeast of Capernaum, in the territory ruled by Philip, a son of Herod the Great, during Jesus' public ministry. Bethsaida was built on a hilltop near where the Jordan River flows into the northern end of the Sea of Galilee, allowing boats to be moored below the village. Archaeologists estimate that the population of Bethsaida at the time of Jesus was several hundred people. Some first-century houses have been discovered. Fishhooks and other fishing gear were found; the name "Bethsaida" may mean "house of the hunter," that is, one who hunts fish. John's Gospel tells us that one of Jesus' disciples, named Philip, "was from Bethsaida, the town of Andrew and Peter" (John

1:44). The other Gospels portray Peter and Andrew living in Capernaum during Jesus' public ministry; perhaps they moved from Bethsaida to Capernaum. Bethsaida was apparently destroyed by an earthquake in A.D. 115; it was ultimately abandoned in the fourth century.

### Peter professed that Jesus was the Messiah near Caesarea Philippi. Where was that?

Caesarea Philippi is not to be confused with Caesarea, a city on the Mediterranean coast that is mentioned in Acts. Caesarea Philippi lay about twenty-five miles north of the Sea of Galilee, in the northern portion of the territory ruled by Philip at the time of Jesus. (Today this region is called the Jaulan or Golan Heights.) The site of Caesarea Philippi had long been a place of pagan worship, centered on a powerful spring that poured forth from the mouth of a cave and was one of the sources of the Jordan River. In the centuries immediately before the time of Jesus the site was dedicated to the Greek nature god Pan and called Paneas. Herod the Great built a temple at Paneas dedicated to the Roman emperor Caesar Augustus. After the death of Herod the Great in 4 B.C., rule over the region northeast of the Sea of Galilee passed to his son Philip. Philip enlarged Paneas, renaming it Caesarea in honor of the Roman emperor. It came to be called "Philip's Caesarea" (Caesarea Philippi) to distinguish it from other cities named in honor of the emperor. At the time of Jesus, Caesarea

Philippi was largely Gentile in population and pagan in religion; only a small minority of Jews lived in the city and nearby villages.

### *Where was Cana, where Jesus transformed water into wine?*

Two sites have been venerated as Cana. From the fourth century until after the crusades, Cana was identified with Khirbet Qana (Ruin of Qana), nine miles north of Nazareth. The site has been partially excavated by archaeologists; they estimate that it had a maximum population of five hundred at the time of Jesus. In the sixteenth century attention shifted to another site with a name similar to Cana: Kefar Kenna (Village of Kenna), four miles northeast of Nazareth. Today Khirbet Qana is a bare hilltop with remains of ancient buildings; Kefar Kenna is a Palestinian town that traditionally has had a largely Christian population. Although Khirbet Qana is likely the site of New Testament Cana, it is more practical for pilgrims to commemorate the events that took place in Cana at Kefar Kenna with its churches and easier access.

### *What was Capernaum, that Jesus should make it his base of operations?*

Capernaum lay on the northwest shore of the Sea of Galilee, along a road that led from the Mediterranean to Bethsaida and ultimately to Damascus. Since Capernaum was near the border between the territory governed by Herod Antipas and the territory governed by his half-brother Philip, there was a customs post there to collect taxes on goods being transported between the territories. Capernaum was a fishing and farming village covering about twenty-five acres, with a population estimated to have been between six hundred and fifteen hundred. Its houses were one story and small by modern standards, with walls of unworked stones and flat thatched roofs. Capernaum was a village of ordinary rural Galileans. There was no evidence of public buildings, other than what seem to be the remains of an earlier synagogue beneath a later fourth or fifth century synagogue. Jesus moved from Nazareth to Capernaum and made Capernaum his base of operations for his public ministry; Mark and Matthew indicate that he stayed in the house of Peter. In later centuries there was a continuing Jewish Christian presence in Capernaum, alongside its Jewish population. Capernaum was progressively abandoned after the seventh-century Islamic conquest of Palestine and an earthquake in 746.

### What do we know about Chorazin at the time of Jesus?

Not much. Chorazin was a small farming village built on a hill two miles north of Capernaum. Although excavated by archaeologists, no significant remains from the time of Jesus have been discovered. Chorazin was destroyed by an earthquake in the fourth century, rebuilt in the fifth century, and abandoned in the ninth century.

## Where was Emmaus, the destination of two disciples after Jesus' resurrection?

Three different sites have been venerated as Emmaus. During the fourth to seventh centuries, Christians identified Emmaus with the Emmaus mentioned in 1 Maccabees (1 Macc 3:40, 57; 4:3; 9:50), even though it was about nineteen miles west of Jerusalem rather than the seven miles (literally, sixty *stadia*) specified by Luke (Luke 24:13; some copyists revised Luke's Gospel to read one hundred sixty *stadia*, which is roughly nineteen miles). This Emmaus, near today's Latrun, was abandoned after a plague in A.D. 639. After the crusaders conquered Jerusalem in 1099, they settled on a site for Emmaus about nine miles west of Jerusalem. This site, at today's Abu Ghosh, was venerated as Emmaus during the crusader era but later fell out of use. Christians visiting the Holy Land thereafter settled on a third site for Emmaus, called Qubeiba today, seven miles northwest of Jerusalem. The Emmaus mentioned by Luke was very likely at a fourth site. At the time of Jesus there was a village named Emmaus three and a half miles west of Jerusalem; Romans changed its name to Colonia later in the first century. The Palestinian village of Qaluniya marked the site until 1948; today it is Motza, a suburb of Jerusalem. When Luke wrote that Emmaus was seven miles from Jerusalem he was apparently referring to a round trip. The chronology of events in chapter 24 of Luke's Gospel works best if Emmaus was only three and a half miles from Jerusalem. The two disciples could have eaten an afternoon meal with Jesus (Luke 24:29–31) and returned to Jerusalem to meet with the other disciples (24:33–35), with there still being time for the risen Jesus to appear to them (24:36–49) and lead them to Bethany (24:50–52).

## What were Gadara and Gerasa?

Gadara and Gerasa were two cities of the Decapolis, a confederation of ten largely Gentile cities chiefly lying east of the Jordan River. Gadara was about five miles southeast of the Sea of Galilee; Gerasa (the city of Jerash in modern Jordan) lies about thirty-three miles southeast of this Sea. Jesus traveled into the general region of these cities — into "the territory of the Gadarenes" according to some ancient Gospel manuscripts (see Matt 8:28) or into "the territory of the Gerasenes" according to other ancient Gospel manuscripts (see Mark 5:1; Luke 8:26). In still other ancient Gospel manuscripts he went into "the territory of the Gergesenes;" the site of Gergesa is unknown. Once in this territory Jesus sent a legion of demons into a herd of swine, which rushed down a steep bank into the Sea of Galilee and drowned (Matt 8:32; Mark 5:13; Luke 8:33). The distance of Gadara and Gerasa from the Sea of Galilee makes it difficult to determine where this took place. Christian tradition dating back at least to the fifth century located it at Kursi, a site on a steep hill rising from the eastern shore of the Sea of Galilee; it could have been part of the territory of Gadara.

## What is notable about Jericho?

Jericho can lay claim to being both the lowest and the oldest city on earth. Jericho lies in the Jordan Valley, ten miles from where the Jordan River empties into the Dead Sea. The city is about 850 feet below sea level (for comparison, Death Valley in the United States is about 280 feet below sea level). Jericho was built at the site of a powerful spring that flows to this day. In ancient Jericho, archaeologists have discovered a thirty-foot-high tower and city walls dating from around 8,000 B.C. — almost seven thousand years before Joshua came along. At the time of Jesus, the tower and the wall had long been buried in a pile of rubble. Jericho lay along one of the most commonly used routes for travel between Galilee and Jerusalem. The road from Jericho to Jerusalem went by a palace that Herod the Great had built to enjoy Jericho's warm winter weather; Jerusalem, only seventeen miles away but twenty-five hundred feet above sea level, is cold and damp in the winter.

## What made Jerusalem important?

Jerusalem lies on rocky hills about twenty-five hundred feet above sea level; hence the Bible speaks of "going up" to Jerusalem and "going down" from Jerusalem. In Old Testament times, Jerusalem's importance was political and religious rather than geographic or economic.

It did not lie on any trade routes nor is the region a lush agricultural area: the eastern outskirts of Jerusalem border on the Judean wilderness. However, David chose Jerusalem to be his capital, and Solomon built the first Israelite Temple there. Jerusalem remained the religious center of the Jews even after they lost political independence. Jerusalem's population at the time of Jesus is estimated to have been around forty thousand. Well over one hundred thousand more people would crowd into the city during the pilgrimage feasts of Passover, Weeks, and Booths. The Temple was the mainstay of Jerusalem's economy, by one estimate accounting for 20 percent of the city's income. The massive revamping of the Temple complex that Herod the Great, which began in 20 B.C. and continued almost until the time of the Jewish revolt in A.D. 66, was a major public-works project. Offerings brought to the Temple and the sale of animals for sacrifice brought income to Jerusalem and to those who controlled the Temple. Jerusalem was a company town, and that company was the Temple.

### What do we know about Magdala, the hometown of Mary Magdalene?

Magdala was a town on the western shore of the Sea of Galilee, about three miles north of Tiberias and seven miles south of Capernaum. It was a center for processing and selling fish caught in the Sea of Galilee. Later Jewish writings call it *Migdal Nunayya*, meaning "fish tower" — likely referring to a tower used for smoking fish. In Greek it was known as *Taricheae*, from a word that means dried, smoked, or pickled fish. Smoking, salting, and pickling fish preserved them for export. Magdala had a harbor and shipyard, making it a center for commerce. One ancient writer characterized Magdala as a place of wealth. Archaeological excavations begun in 2009 have uncovered the remains of a first-century synagogue as well as of substantial houses, a market, and a fisherman's work area. It is a reasonable conjecture that when Jesus traveled about teaching in synagogues (Matt 4:23; 9:35; Mark 1:39; Luke 4:15, 44; John 18:20), he visited the synagogue of Magdala. At least one of his followers came from there: Mary of Magdala, better known as Mary Magdalene.

### *Where is Nain mentioned in Scripture?*

The only reference to Nain in Scripture is found in the Gospel of Luke, which recounts that Jesus restored the life of a widow's only son who had died (Luke 7:11–17). Nain lies about six miles southeast of Nazareth; today it is a small Palestinian village in the state of Israel. No significant remains of first-century buildings have been discovered.

### *What was noteworthy about Nazareth, the village in which Jesus spent most of his life?*

Nazareth was an insignificant farming village located on a hillside overlooking the Jezreel Valley in southern Galilee. The remains of ancient Nazareth lie beneath the modern town of Nazareth and have been only partially excavated. An archaeologist concluded that the village sat on about four acres of land and had fewer than fifty houses, with a population of about three hundred, the majority of them children. Remains from the first century indicate that houses in Nazareth had fieldstone walls and thatched roofs. No luxury items have been found on the site. Nazareth is not mentioned in the Old Testament; its unimportance is reflected in Nathanael's question, "Can anything good come from Nazareth?" (John 1:46). There was apparently nothing to distinguish Nazareth from other small farming villages in Galilee during the years Jesus called it home.

## What was Sepphoris?

Although Sepphoris lay only four miles from Nazareth and was the capital of Galilee for roughly the first half of Jesus' life, it is never mentioned in the New Testament. Sepphoris was already an important city as the Old Testament era came to an end. Rome took control of Palestine in the middle of the first century B.C. and made Sepphoris the seat of the regional government. When Herod the Great came to power, he retained Sepphoris as his northern capital. After Herod died in 4 B.C., the people of Sepphoris joined a revolt to win independence from Roman and Herodian rule. Rome put down the revolt, destroying Sepphoris in the process. Herod Antipas, a son of Herod the great, inherited rule of Galilee and rebuilt Sepphoris as his capital. While there are speculations that Jesus worked as a carpenter in the rebuilding of Sepphoris, there is no evidence that he did so. There are some archaeological indications of a cultural divide between Sepphoris and Nazareth, with Nazareth exhibiting a traditional lifestyle and Sepphoris a more cosmopolitan one. The Gospels never recount Jesus visiting Sepphoris, and his parables largely reflect a simple rural lifestyle. Between A.D. 17 and 20, Herod Antipas built the city of Tiberias on the shore of the Sea of Galilee as a new capital for himself, but Sepphoris remained an important and growing city.

### What was Tiberias?

Herod Antipas inherited Sepphoris as a capital city for Galilee from his father, Herod the Great, even though he had to rebuild it. Antipas apparently wanted to replace Sepphoris with a capital that was entirely his own. He built a new city on the southwest shore of the Sea of Galilee, dedicating it in A.D. 20 and naming it Tiberias in honor of the reigning Roman emperor. The city incorporated features found in cosmopolitan Greek cities of the time, including hot baths and a stadium. In the course of construction a cemetery was discovered on the site, making the land unclean for Jews and unsuitable for dwellings. Consequently Herod Antipas had to compel Jews to live there, and he filled out the population of Tiberias with Gentiles. Tiberias lay only seven miles from Capernaum, but the Gospels do not recount

Jesus ever visiting Tiberias. Luke's Gospel tells of some women who provided for Jesus and his disciples out of their resources, and it names three of the women, including Mary from Magdala, a city two miles from Tiberias, and "Joanna, the wife of Herod's steward Chuza" (Luke 8:2–3). As the chief administrator for Herod Antipas, Chuza likely had to live in Tiberias. Jesus attracted at least one follower — Joanna — from Tiberias, even if he may have avoided the city itself.

## Where are Tyre and Sidon?

Tyre and Sidon were the largest cities in southern Phoenicia, the Mediterranean coastal region northwest of Galilee. Both cities, lying in what is today's Lebanon, were seaports and trading centers. Tyre was about 35 miles northwest of the Sea of Galilee; Sidon lay about 22 miles up the coast from Tyre. Lands under the control of Tyre and Sidon extended east and south toward Galilee. Galilee provided grain and other crops to Tyre and Sidon in both Old and New Testament times (see Ezek 27:17; Acts 12:20). The populations of Tyre and Sidon were predominantly Gentile with a Jewish minority. The Church took root in Tyre and Sidon within a few decades of the resurrection of Jesus (see Acts 21:3–6; 27:3).

# 4

# THE JEWISH WORLD
# OF JESUS

### What are alms?

Alms are money given to help those in need. A clue to the meaning of "alms" is found in the Greek word used in the Gospels for "alms," for it is derived from the verb that means to show mercy (the English word "alms" is derived from the same Greek word). There is no mention of giving alms in the early Old Testament era, because money had not yet been invented. In a farming economy, mercy could be exercised by feeding the hungry with what one raised or letting the poor glean crops from one's fields (Lev 19:9-10; Deut 15:11). As coins came into use, the hungry could be also helped by giving them money to buy food and to meet their other needs. Almsgiving — the showing of mercy by giving money — is praised in the books of Tobit (Tobit 4:7-11, 16; 12:8-9) and Sirach (Sirach 3:29; 7:10), among the last books of the Old Testament to be written.

### *What does the Bible tell us about angels?*

The Hebrew and Greek words translated as "angel" also mean "messenger," and angels appear in early Old Testament writings as messengers of God. These messengers are not always clearly distinguished from manifestations of God himself (Gen 16:7–13; Exod 3:2–6). Some Scripture passages speak of members of God's heavenly court, sometimes calling them "the sons of God," meaning "heavenly beings" (Job 1:6), or calling them the "host," or army, "of heaven" (1 Kings 22:19–22), an expression that can also refer to stars (Deut 4:19). Cherubim are heavenly beings, too (Ezek 10:18–20; see also Gen 3:24), as are seraphim (Isaiah 6:2). Thus the Old Testament speaks of a variety of heavenly beings without relating them to one another, without calling all of them angels, and without defining their nature. Individual angels are not named until late Old Testament writings. Raphael (Tobit 5:4; 12:15), Gabriel (Dan 8:15–16; 9:21), and Michael (Dan 10:13) are the only three angels named in the Old Testament. Michael, the prince or guardian angel of God's people (Dan 12:1), contends with other heavenly beings who are the guardians of other nations (Dan 10:13, 20–21). Speculations about angels multiplied late in the Old Testament era and are reflected in Jewish writings that did not become part of Scripture. The perplexing account in Genesis of "the sons of heaven," literally, "sons of God" (see Job 1:6) who had intercourse with women (Gen 6:1–4), developed into a story of the fall of some angels who led humans into sin. The chief of the fallen angels was given various names, including "Satan." At the time of Jesus, angels were generally thought of as human in form (2 Macc 3:25–26; Dan 8:15–16) but with heavenly rather than earthly bodies, not needing to eat or drink (Tobit 12:19).

## What is baptism?

The Greek word for baptize means to dip, plunge, immerse, drench, soak, or wash. Mark uses a variant of this word to describe the washing of dishes (Mark 7:4). There is some indication that John's baptism involved fully immersing a person in water: John 3:23 suggests that John needed ample water, and Mark 1:10 speaks of Jesus "coming up out of the water" after being baptized. In Matthew's Gospel, after his resurrection Jesus directs his disciples to "make disciples of all nations, baptizing them in the name of the Father, and of the Son, and of the holy Spirit" (Matt 28:19). In Acts, Peter exhorts the crowd that gathered on Pentecost to "repent and be baptized, every one of you, in the name of Jesus Christ for the forgiveness of your sins; and you will receive the gift of the holy Spirit" (Acts 2:38). Christian baptism is "the bath of rebirth / and renewal by the holy Spirit" (Titus 3:5) that allows one to enter the kingdom of God (John 3:5).

## What is the meaning of beatitudes and woes?

A beatitude praises or congratulates someone for being fortunate, telling why or how they are fortunate.

"A woman from the crowd called out and said to him, 'Blessed is the womb that carried you and the breasts at which you nursed.' He replied, 'Rather, blessed are those who hear the word of God and observe it'" (Luke 11:27–28). There are about sixty beatitudes in the Old Testament and, by one count, twenty-eight in the New Testament. Psalm 1 is an extended beatitude. It begins with an exclamation, "Happy the man," or "person," and then lays out the basis of the person's happiness: he or she avoids bad company, does what is right, and spends time meditating on Scripture (Psalm 1:1–2). For the listener, a beatitude encourages the behavior that is the basis of the blessed person's happiness. Beatitudes may also describe the nature of the person's happiness. Psalm 1, for example, speaks of flourishing even in difficult circumstances (Psalm 1:3). Beatitudes are sometimes translated, "Blessed is so and so," but a beatitude does not call down God's blessing on a person; it declares that the person is already blessed by God and can look forward to the happiness God has in mind for him or her because of their way of being or doing.

A woe is the opposite of a beatitude. While a beatitude congratulates someone as fortunate, a woe laments and reproaches someone for his or her unfortunate condition. Just as a beatitude encourages the behavior that is being praised, a woe warns against the behavior that is being lamented. There are about fifty woes in the Old Testament, mostly as prophetic denunciations of those who do evil. Chapter

5 of Isaiah pronounces six woes: "Woe to those who call evil good, and good evil" (Isaiah 5:20; see also 5:8, 11, 18, 21–22). The New Testament has thirty-seven woes. Luke's Gospel pairs four beatitudes with four woes (Luke 6:20–26). A woe is a cry of grief and alarm over a course of action that will bring God's punishment (see Matt 11:20–24). Woes are warnings and expressions of sorrow, not curses.

## Who is Beelzebul?

Jesus is sometimes accused of being an agent of Beelzebul in the Gospels. Scholars debate the meaning of the name "Beelzebul." One suggestion is that it is an ancient name for the Canaanite god Baal. While there is no certainty about the origin of the name, in the New Testament Beelzebul clearly is another name for Satan, "the prince of demons" (Matt 12:24).

## What do clean and unclean refer to?

The Old Testament contains complex regulations regarding the ritually clean and the ritually unclean, for example, Leviticus 11–15. The ritually clean could come in contact with the holy; the ritually unclean could not. An unclean person could not worship in the Temple. A person could become unclean either through sin or through a variety of causes that had nothing to do with sin. Sexual intercourse, even if perfectly moral, rendered one unclean, as did menstruation or giving birth to a child. Uncleanness also resulted from certain diseases or contact with a corpse. In these cases, contact with an unclean person or object rendered a person unclean. An unclean person could be made clean through remedies that depended on the type of uncleanness. Washing with water and the passage of a certain amount of time were required, and, for more serious types of uncleanness, sacrifice in the Temple. Most Jews were probably ritually unclean much of the time but could remedy their condition in order to enter the Temple area (see John 11:55). Maintaining or restoring cleanness was important for priests because they served in the Temple, and special rules pertained to them. Ritual cleanness was a particular concern for the Pharisees, and their program aimed at maintaining in everyday life the ritual purity required for Temple worship. Archaeologists have found widespread evidence of concern for ritual cleanness in Galilee and Judea (baths for ritual washing; cups and bowls carved from stone, which was impervious to uncleanness — see John 2:6), but most Jews of Jesus' time did not observe the detailed traditions of the Pharisees.

### What are the Dead Sea Scrolls and why are they important?

In 1947, a Bedouin shepherd boy came across some clay jars in a cave overlooking the Dead Sea. The jars contained seven ancient scrolls, including the book of Isaiah. Over the next nine years more scrolls were found in ten other caves in the area. Over nine hundred different scrolls have been discovered, virtually all of them incomplete and decayed, in more than one hundred thousand fragments. The process of assembling and translating the fragments has taken scholars many years. The scrolls were copied between roughly 200 B.C. and A.D. 68 and represent an entire library. About two hundred of the scrolls were copies of books of the Old Testament, including thirty-six copies of the Psalms. Also discovered were copies of nonbiblical religious writings, including about ten copies of *1 Enoch* and fifteen copies of *Jubilees*, as well as scrolls of religious writings that had been previously unknown to modern scholars. Along with these works, which had been in general circulation among Jews at the time of Jesus, were a number of works that pertained to the religious community that owned the library. Some of these scrolls were community rules, hymns used in the community, and commentaries on books of the Old Testament written from the community's perspective. The community that owned this library is commonly identified as the Essenes, a sect headquartered at Qumran, on the shore of the Dead Sea, where the scrolls were found.

### What are demons or unclean spirits?

The New Testament takes the existence of demons for granted and does not describe their origin or say much about their nature. The chief emphasis lies on their influence and effects on human beings. Both mental and physical illnesses, including epilepsy, blindness, deafness, muteness, and curvature of the spine, are sometimes ascribed to the influence of demons, and healing takes place through casting out the demon causing the illness. But not every illness is attributed to the influence of demons, and some healings are presented simply as cures. Likewise, some exorcisms are simply exorcisms, with no mention of any accompanying physical healing. Demons are also referred to as unclean spirits and evil spirits, and they are under the authority of Satan, also called Beelzebul.

### *What was involved in fasting?*

In both the Old and New Testaments, fasting means abstaining from all food for a period of time. In its origins, fasting may have been a sign of mourning: David fasted following the deaths of Saul, Jonathan, and Abner (2 Sam 1:12; 3:31–35), and Judith fasted after the death of her husband as part of her mourning (Judith 8:2–6). Fasting out of grief was not necessarily a religious practice but a mark that one was so deeply sorrowful that he or she had lost all appetite for food. Fasting as an expression of sorrow may have evolved to include fasting as an expression of sorrow for sin (Joel 2:12–13). The Day of Atonement is the only annual fast day prescribed in the law of Moses (Lev 16:29). Fasts could also be called in times of national crisis, as part of prayers of supplication (Joel 1:14). Prophets such as Isaiah warned that fasting was no substitute for upright and merciful conduct (Isaiah 58). Eventually fasting became a pious act, done not only in times of sorrow or crisis but also simply as an act of devotion. The book of Tobit, written about two centuries before Jesus, lists fasting, prayer, and almsgiving as three pious Jewish practices (Tobit 12:8). Different Jewish groups at the time of Jesus had their own traditions of fasting. The *Didache,* a Christian writing dating from about a century after Jesus, speaks of Jews fasting on Mondays and Thursdays and advises Christians to fast instead on Wednesdays and Fridays.

## What did the feast of the Dedication commemorate?

Commonly known as Hanukkah, the eight-day feast of the Dedication commemorated Jewish independence from Syria and the reconsecration of the Temple in 164 B.C. Palestine had been under the rule of Antiochus IV Epiphanes, whose capital was Antioch, in present-day Turkey. In an attempt to unify his empire, Antiochus suppressed Jewish religious practices and imposed the worship of Greek gods (1 Macc 1:41–63; 2 Macc 6:1–11). In 167 B.C., Antiochus erected an altar to the Olympian Zeus over the altar of the Temple (2 Macc 6:2); 1 Maccabees calls this altar "the desolating abomination" (1 Macc 1:54; see Dan 9:27; 11:31; Matt 24:15; Mark 13:14). Jews revolted against Antiochus and won independence under the leadership of Judas Maccabeus. He ordered that the altar to Zeus be demolished and the Temple purified (1 Macc 4:36–51; 2 Macc 10:1–4). The Temple was re-consecrated in 164 B.C., with an eight-day celebration (1 Macc 4:52–58; 2 Macc 10:5–7). This celebration was repeated as an annual feast (1 Macc 4:59; 2 Macc 10:8), with Jews in other lands invited to join in its celebration (2 Macc 1:18).

### How were the feasts of Passover and Unleavened Bread related to each other?

The feasts of Passover and Unleavened Bread originated as different feasts but were celebrated in conjunction with each other. Both feasts incorporated traditions of nomadic shepherds and settled farmers but took on greater meaning as part of a celebration of the liberation from Egypt (see Exod 13:3–10; 23:15; 34:18). Passover was celebrated by a meal that included lamb; it commemorated God's freeing the Israelites from captivity in Egypt (Exod 12). Some scholars believe than an ancient precursor of Passover was the sacrifice of a young lamb as an offering for the safety of the flock, made by shepherds in the spring before moving the flock to new pastures. The Passover meal was eaten with unleavened bread after sundown on the fourteenth day of the spring month of Nisan (also called Abib) — a night of a full moon in the lunar calendar followed by Jews. The seven-day celebration of the feast of Unleavened Bread began at the same time (Lev 23:5–6; Deut 16:1–8). This feast was a springtime agricultural festival celebrating the beginning of the grain harvest. In Palestine during biblical times, grain crops grew only during the winter rainy season, with barley being the first grain to ripen in the spring. To celebrate the barley harvest, bread made only from newly harvested grain was eaten for seven days. This bread was unleavened because leaven was in the form of starter dough, and no starter dough from previously harvested grain could be used during this feast (Exod 12:18–20). After sacrificial worship was restricted to the Temple in Jerusalem by King Josiah (ruled 640–609 B.C.), Passover was celebrated only in Jerusalem, since the sacrificing of lambs had to be done at the Temple.

### What did the feast of Tabernacles celebrate?

In its ancient origins the feast of Tabernacles, also called the feast of Booths (Lev 23:34; Deut 16:13), was a fall agricultural festival, celebrating the harvest of fruit crops, especially grapes and olives, that ripened over the summer. The feast takes its name from the practice of erecting temporary huts in orchards and vineyards for harvesters to sleep in at night, guarding the ripened crops. The feast is also known as the feast of Ingathering (Exod 23:16; 34:22), reflecting its nature as a harvest festival. Historical associations were added to the agricultural feast so that it became a commemoration of Israel's forty-year sojourn in the desert, a time in which the people lived in booths or temporary shelters (Lev 23:42–43). After sacrificial worship was centralized at the Temple in Jerusalem, the feast of Tabernacles became a pilgrimage feast celebrated in Jerusalem (Exod 23:14–17; 34:22–24; Deut 16:16). The feast lasted seven days (Lev 23:34; Num 29:12; Deut 16:13–15), during which time men slept at night in temporary booths (Lev 23:42; Neh 8:13–18). The feast concluded with a solemn assembly on the eighth day of (Lev 23:36; Num 29:35; Neh 8:18). Since the feast occurred shortly before the beginning of the winter rainy season, it became an occasion for praying for the rain necessary for grain crops, which are grown in Palestine during the winter. The Temple was illuminated with torches at night during the feast of Tabernacles, allowing celebrations to continue after dark. The first-century Jewish historian Josephus wrote that Tabernacles was the most popular of the annual Jewish feasts.

### What is God's name?

The English word "God" is the generic term for the Supreme Being, and the Hebrew portions of the Old Testament use an equivalent generic term for God. The Old Testament, however, also uses the personal name for God, which in Hebrew is written with letters that correspond to the English letters YHWH. The Hebrew letters represent a unique form of the verb "to be." Biblical Hebrew was written largely without vowels, and thus it is impossible to be certain how this name was pronounced; it may have been pronounced "Yahweh." The Old Testament presents God revealing his name, *YHWH*, to Moses at the burning bush (Exod 3:15). Out of reverence, Jews in the time of Jesus, as still today, avoided saying the name of God; when they read Scripture aloud and came to the name *YHWH,* they substituted a Hebrew word for "Lord." When the Hebrew Scriptures were translated into Greek, the Greek word for Lord was used to translate *YHWH.* The Old Testament of the *New American Bible* uses the word "Lord," printed with large and small capitals, and on rare occasions "God," to stand for the Hebrew *YHWH.*

### How much religious diversity was there among Jews at the time of Jesus?

While all Jews at the time of Jesus shared certain fundamental beliefs and observances, there was considerable diversity when it came to specific views and practices. All Jews revered the law of Moses and the Temple, but different groups, such as the Pharisees, Sadducees, and Essenes, developed different traditions for observing the law. These groups also had differing views on such matters as the kind of messiah or messiahs God would send and whether there would be an afterlife or resurrection of the dead. The vast majority of Jews belonged to no religious group or party. Pharisees, the largest and most influential party, numbered only about six thousand. There were also degrees of compliance with God's laws, however these laws were interpreted. Zealous groups, such as the Pharisees and Essenes, developed and followed traditions for strictly living out God's laws. On the other end of the spectrum were those universally considered sinners because they violated some of God's basic commands. Most Jews fell somewhere in the middle, observing the law as best as their circumstances allowed but without adopting the practices of the Pharisees. The Judaism of today has roots in the Pharisees of the time of Jesus but reflects a considerable development of traditions and practices.

### How do nonbiblical writings form part of the background for understanding the teachings of Jesus?

Other religious writings besides the books of the Old Testament were in circulation among Jews at the time of Jesus. Many of these texts had been written in the previous two centuries. Two of these writings, *1 Enoch* and the *Assumption of Moses,* are quoted in the letter of Jude (Jude 6, 9, 14–15). Other writings included *Jubilees, Psalms of Solomon,* and some of the *Testaments of the Twelve Patriarchs,* as well as other writings found among the Dead Sea Scrolls. Some of these writings claim to be revelations of how God will act to overcome evil and begin a new age. They differ considerably over what lies ahead. Various ideas about messianic figures, angels, the present age and the age to come, judgment, the resurrection of the dead, and life in the age to come are found in these writings, in more developed forms than they are found in the books of the Old Testament. It is uncertain how popular each of these writings was at the time of Jesus or how familiar the average Jew was with them. Yet at least some of their ideas and imagery, such as of Gehenna as a place of fiery punishment, were sufficiently familiar to first-century Jews for Jesus to invoke them in his teachings without having to explain them as if his listeners were hearing of them for the first time. These writings form part of the background for the Gospels and help bridge the Old and the New Testaments, even though they are not part of inspired Scripture.

### Jesus liked to teach in parables — did he invent the idea of a parable?

Jesus did not invent the idea of conveying a message by means of a parable (see 2 Sam 12:1–7 for an Old Testament example; parables are also found in ancient Greek literature). The Greek word for parable contains elements that mean "setting beside," "placing side by side," thus a comparison or illustration. The Hebrew word translated as "parable" has a broad range of meanings, including "proverb," "riddle," "metaphor," "story," "fable," and "allegory." Jesus' parables range from pithy sayings ("No one pours new wine into old wineskins" — Mark 2:22) to miniature stories (the parable of the loving father — Luke 15:11–32). Jesus' parables often use features of everyday life as terms of comparison that throw light on what God is doing through him or how one should respond to what God is doing. Jesus' parables are vivid but sometimes enigmatic. They are meant to be thought provoking, to stimulate the listener's reflection. Sometimes they confront the listener with a decision: Make up your mind — where do you stand? Some scholars have claimed that each parable makes only one point, but that is an artificial restriction. Some parables are like diamonds, revealing new facets of meaning when examined from different angles. The Greek word for parable is not used in the Gospel of John, which calls the comparisons that Jesus makes "figures of speech" — enigmatic sayings (John 10:6; 16:25, 29).

## What are phylacteries?

Phylacteries are small leather boxes containing Scripture passages on pieces of parchment, bound with straps to the forehead and left arm. In Deuteronomy God enjoins his people to "take to heart these words which I enjoin on you today.... Bind them at your wrist as a sign and let them be as a pendant on your forehead" (Deut 6:6, 8; see also Exod 13:9, 16; Deut 11:18). Devout Jews began to wear phylacteries several centuries before the time of Jesus as an observance of this command. The Scripture passages placed in phylacteries are Exod 13:1–16 and Deut 6:4–9; 11:13–21; some first-century phylacteries also contained a copy of the Ten Commandments. Phylacteries are not mentioned in the Old Testament, and in the New Testament only in Matthew 23:5.

### What are the Psalms of Solomon *and what do they have to say about the Messiah?*

Eighteen hymns called the *Psalms of Solomon* were written around 50 B.C., probably in Jerusalem. While not part of Scripture, they shed light on the messianic expectations of some Jews around the time of Jesus. One psalm speaks of a messiah who will deliver Jews from Roman rule and lead them into holiness: "See, Lord, and raise up for them their king, the son of David, to rule over your servant Israel in the time you have chosen, O God. Gird him with strength to shatter unrighteous rulers, to cleanse Jerusalem from gentiles who trample and destroy it,... to destroy their sinful pride like a clay pot, to smash their plan with an iron rod.... He will have gentile nations serving under his yoke ... and he will cleanse Jerusalem and make it holy as it was in the beginning.... For all shall be holy, and their king shall be the Lord Messiah. He will not trust in horse and rider and bow; he will not multiply gold and silver for war.... He himself will be free from sin so as to rule over a great people. He will put officials to shame and drive out sinners by the strength of a word. And he will not weaken during his days, because of his God, for God has made him powerful with a holy spirit.... This is the majesty of the king of Israel, whom God knew, to raise him over the house of Israel" (*Psalms of Solomon* 17:21–24, 30, 32–33, 36–37,

42). The "Lord Messiah" of this psalm, while sinless, is a human being, and his rule takes place on this earth.

### What does it mean to call someone a rabbi?

The Hebrew word *rab* means "great"; with a first-person possessive ending it becomes *rabbi*, "my great one." The word "rabbi" is not found in the Old Testament, but had become a deferential form of address by the time of Jesus. Eventually this respectful form of address came to be used as a title for those with teaching authority within Judaism, which is the meaning that the title "rabbi" has today. This later meaning is reflected in Gospel passages where "rabbi" is equated with "teacher" (Matt 23:8; John 1:38; 3:2).

### What are the Old and New Testaments' understandings of repentance?

In the Old Testament, the Hebrew word used for "repent" means to turn back or return: "Return, O Israel, to the LORD, your God" (Hosea 14:2). The New Testament expresses repentance differently: the Greek word translated "repentance" literally means "a change of mind." A change of mind means recognizing that one's views are wrong or inadequate. If wrong views lead to wrong actions, then a change of mind should result in a change of behavior. Summing up all of this is the notion of conversion, a profound reorientation of oneself. When John the Baptist and Jesus call for repentance, they are calling for an acceptance of the messages they proclaim and for life changes on the basis of their messages. Repentance is not simply a matter of feeling sorry but also of adopting new attitudes and new behavior.

### What is the meaning of the Sabbath?

The Sabbath is the seventh day of the week in the Jewish calendar, our Saturday. "Sabbath" comes from a Hebrew verb that means to stop or cease, indicating an essential note of the Sabbath: it was a day on which all work was to cease. The third of the Ten Commandments spells this out: "Remember the sabbath day — keep it holy. Six days you may labor and do all your work, but the seventh day is a sabbath of the LORD your God. You shall not do any work, either you, your son or your daughter, your male or female slave, your work animal, or the resident alien within your gates" (Exod 20:8–10). Eventually the Sabbath became a day for prayer and study of Scripture as well as a day of rest. By the time of Jesus, complex interpretations had been developed of what constituted work forbidden on the Sabbath — for example, walking more than roughly one thousand yards (the "sabbath day's journey" of Acts 1:12). Different Jewish groups had different interpretations of what constituted forbidden work, with some Pharisees taking a very rigorous approach. Jesus proclaimed his authority to teach on behalf of God how the Sabbath should be observed (Matt 12:8; Mark 2:28; Luke 6:5; see also John 5:16–30). He rejected rigorous Sabbath regulations as burdensome and instead emphasized the original meaning of the Sabbath, a day of rest and restoration that God had given to his people (see Mark 2:27; 3:4; Luke 13:16; 14:5; John 7:23).

## Who is Satan?

In Hebrew, the word *satan* means "adversary" (in a military or political sense) or "accuser" (in a legal sense). A figure called "the Satan," that is, "the accuser," appears in the book of Job as an angelic prosecuting attorney who puts humans to the test (Job 1:6–12; 2:1–7). In Job this accuser is a member of God's heavenly court, not an evil spirit opposed to God (see also Zech 3:1–2). In late Old Testament times, however, the term "Satan" began to be applied to an evil spirit (see 1 Chron 21:1). Jewish nonbiblical writings from shortly before the time of Jesus describe the fall of some angels, the chief of whom is variously called Mastema, Satan, Belial, and Beliar. In the New Testament, this evil spirit is likewise called a variety of names, including "Satan," "the devil," "Beelzebul," and "Beliar" and is portrayed as the chief of evil spirits (Matt 12:24–27; Mark 3:22; Luke 11:15–19; 2 Cor 6:15). While demons are inferior to God, they can influence or control individuals and events. The Gospels present Satan as having authority in this world but do not specify its extent (Matt 4:8–9; Luke 4:5–6; John 12:31; 14:30; 16:11; see also 1 John 5:19). The coming of God's kingdom abolishes the sway of Satan. While the kingdom is coming, it is not completely here yet, so there is still evil in the world.

## What does Scripture tell us about the Spirit?

The opening verses of the Old Testament speak of a "mighty wind" (Gen 1:2) that sweeps over the waters as God begins his work of creation. The phrase translated "mighty wind" might also be translated "Spirit of God," for the same Hebrew word means "wind," "breath," or "spirit," and the Hebrew word taken to mean "mighty" can be translated as "divine" or "of God." It is the breath of God breathed into humans that gives life (Gen 2:7). When the Old Testament speaks of the Spirit of God, it generally refers to God's influence or power at work, for example, in the inspiration of prophets (Isaiah 61:1). In the Old Testament the Spirit of God is not yet thought of as a person. The New Testament bears witness to a deeper experience and understanding of the Spirit. Paul speaks of the Spirit many times in his letters (for example, Rom 8) but writes more about what the Spirit does than who the Spirit is. In the Gospel of John, Jesus speaks of the Spirit as the Paraclete, or Advocate, who will carry on his work (John 14:16-7, 26; 15:26; 16:7-11). The Gospel of Matthew ends with Jesus' instruction that people be baptized "in the name of the Father, and of the Son, and of the holy Spirit" (Matt 28:19). The Council of Constantinople in A.D. 381 proclaimed the Spirit to be "the holy, the lordly and life-giving one, proceeding forth from the Father, co-worshipped and co-glorified with Father and Son, the one who spoke through the prophets."

## What is the origin of the synagogue?

The original meaning of the Greek word *synagogue* was a gathering or an assembly, but it came to mean the place of assembly — the building that served as a Jewish community center and place of prayer and study. Synagogues may have originated during the exile in Babylonia, when Israelites were deprived of Temple worship. At the time of Jesus, synagogues, at least in the sense of assemblies, were common in Galilee, in Jerusalem, and wherever Jews resided outside of Palestine. Synagogues were used for Scripture reading and prayer; sacrifices were offered only in the Temple in Jerusalem. Synagogues were also used for religious education and community gatherings, which sometimes included communal meals. After the time of Jesus, synagogues became more exclusively used for religious activities and less as general-purpose community centers. Archaeologists have discovered the remains of a few first-century synagogues. They typically consisted of a large room with tiers of stone benches around the walls. Anything done in such a synagogue — such as Jesus' teachings, healings, and exorcisms — would have been visible to the whole congregation. Remains of a synagogue built of limestone around the fourth century can be seen in Capernaum today. Beneath it are what seem to be the remains of a first-century synagogue built of basalt blocks — apparently the synagogue in which Jesus taught and healed. Remains of another first-century synagogue have been found at the site of Magdala, home of Mary Magdalene.

### What was the Temple and why was it so important?

In the ancient Near East, a temple was thought of as the "house" or "palace" of God. Solomon, who ruled from about 970 to 931 B.C., built the first Israelite Temple in Jerusalem. From the time of King Josiah, who ruled from about 640 to 609 B.C., this Jerusalem Temple was the only site where Jews could offer animal sacrifices. Solomon's Temple was destroyed by the Babylonians in 586 B.C. A second Temple was built after the exile and dedicated in 515 B.C. Herod the Great refurbished this second Temple, enlarging the surrounding courtyard to more than thirty-five acres. Around the perimeter of the courtyard, Herod erected magnificent colonnaded halls similar to structures found elsewhere in the Greek and Roman world. The Temple itself was not a huge building; the precedent established by Solomon's Temple limited its interior floor plan to about 30 by 90 feet (see 1 Kings 6:2). But Herod added auxiliary rooms and a grand entrance, substantially increased the height of the façade of the structure, and plated its exterior with gold. Worshippers gathered outside the Temple rather than within it. An altar for offering burnt sacrifices stood in a courtyard reserved for priests that was in front of — east of — the Temple. East of the Court of

Priests was a small Court of Israel, which ritually clean Jewish men could enter, and to its east was a Court of the Women for ritually clean Jews of any age or sex. The remaining, and by far the largest, portion of the Temple area was a Court of the Gentiles, available to both Jews and non-Jews. The open spaces and colonnaded halls in the Court of the Gentiles provided places for meetings, instruction, the selling of animals for sacrifice, and the changing of coins for Temple taxes and offerings. The Temple also served as a national religious treasury and depository for savings (see 2 Macc 3:5–12). Rome destroyed the Temple in A.D. 70 while putting down a Jewish revolt. It was never rebuilt.

### *What did Jews understand as wisdom?*

In the Old Testament, wisdom is the ability to discern and judge properly and to lead a successful life. Wisdom is a gift from God, the source of wisdom (Prov 2:6; Sirach 1:1). Some Old Testament writings speak of God's wisdom as if it were a person — a woman, perhaps because the Hebrew and Greek words for wisdom are a feminine noun: "Wisdom cries aloud in the street, in the open squares she raises her voice" (Prov 1:20; see also Sirach 4:11–19). Wisdom is presented as the first of God's creations: "Before all ages, in the beginning, he created me, and through all ages I shall not cease to be" (Sirach 24:9; see also Prov 8:22–26). Wisdom assisted God in creating the world (Prov 3:19; see also Wisd 9:9). The Book of Proverbs portrays wisdom as God's "craftsman" in the work of creation (Prov 8:27–30). Jesus' contemporaries would have been familiar with this view of wisdom as God's agent. The early Church understood Jesus Christ in light of the Old Testament view of wisdom when it proclaimed that it was through him that God created the universe (1 Cor 8:6; Col 1:15–16; Heb 1:2; 2:10; Rev 3:14). This view of wisdom is also the background for John's writing, "In the beginning was the Word.... All things came to be through him, and without him nothing came to be" (John 1:1, 3).

# 5

# THE PEOPLE IN JESUS' WORLD

### Who was Annas?

Annas was appointed to be the high priest by the Roman governor in A.D. 6 and he remained high priest until A.D. 15. He continued to be very influential after his term as high priest, and five of his sons, a son-in-law, and a grandson served as the high priest after him. The son-in-law was Caiaphas (John 18:13), the high priest at the time of Jesus' public ministry and death. Some later Jewish writings characterize the priestly dynasty of Annas as greedy and corrupt.

### What does it mean that Jesus appointed twelve apostles?

The English word "apostle" is derived from a Greek word meaning to send out. In secular usage, an apostle was an ambassador or a messenger. Jesus was sent by God (Mark 9:37; John 20:21), and so the letter to the Hebrews calls Jesus an apostle (Heb 3:1). Jesus in turn sent out twelve specifically chosen followers as his envoys, commissioned to bear his message and carry out his work. The Gospels often refer to this group as "the Twelve"; their significance lay in their being a symbol of Jesus' restoration of all Israel, which was made up of twelve tribes (see Luke 22:29–30). The early Church used the term "apostle" for a select few of those who went out on mission for Christ (Rom 1:1; 16:7).

### Did Jesus have brothers and sisters?

Brothers of Jesus are mentioned in the Gospels as well as in Acts 1:14, 1 Corinthians 9:5, and Galatians 1:19. Four brothers are listed by name in Matthew 13:55 and Mark 6:3: James, Joses (or Joseph), Simon, and Judas; unnamed sisters are mentioned in Matthew 13:56 and Mark 6:3. While these references might be interpreted to mean that Mary and Joseph had children after Jesus' birth, other passages seem to indicate a different Mary as the mother of James and Joses (Matt 27:56; Mark 15:40), and the Church from early times has held to the perpetual virginity of Mary. One explanation, circulated in the second-century books *Protoevangelium of James* and *Infancy Gospel of Thomas,* is that the brothers and sisters of Jesus were children of Joseph from a previous marriage; this is the accepted view in the Byzantine and Orthodox tradition. St. Jerome (342–420) proposed that the brothers of Jesus were his cousins, since the Hebrew word for brother can also mean "cousin." Jerome's explanation became widely, but not universally, accepted (Greek has a word for cousin, used in Col 4:10 — "Mark the cousin of Barnabas"). Some of the Gospels present the brothers of Jesus as having no faith in him during his public ministry (Mark 3:21; John 7:3–8). But "Mary the mother of Jesus, and his brothers," awaited Pentecost in the upper room (Acts 1:13–14). Paul lists a James, apparently the James called "the brother of the Lord" (Gal 1:19), who was not one of the twelve apostles, as among those to whom Jesus appeared after his resurrection (1 Cor 15:7). "James the brother of the Lord" (Gal 1:19) emerged as the leader of the Christian community in Jerusalem (Acts 12:17; 15:13–21; 21:18; Gal 2:9, 12). New Testament letters are attributed to James (James 1:1) and to his brother Judas (or Jude — Jude 1:1).

## *Who was Caiaphas?*

Caiaphas was high priest from A.D. 18 to 36 — a long time for one man to hold this office. Caiaphas had good connections: his father-in-law was Annas, who served as high priest from A.D. 6 to 15 and used his influence to obtain the high priesthood for five of his sons as well as for Caiaphas. More important, Caiaphas maintained a good relationship with the Roman prefects who governed Judea. These Roman governors appointed the high priest and could remove him from office at any time. In particular, Caiaphas seems to have cooperated with Pilate (who governed Judea from about A.D. 26 to 36), despite Pilate's lack of sensitivity to Jewish religious concerns. Caiaphas may have been responsible for moving the sale of sacrificial animals into the Temple precincts. In any case, he profited from these commercial activities. Jesus' disruption of this commerce and talk of the Temple's destruction would have been reasons for Caiaphas to ask Pilate to get rid of Jesus. What are apparently the tomb and bones of Caiaphas were discovered by archaeologists in 1990; the bones are of a man who died in his sixties.

### What was a centurion?

A centurion was an army officer who usually commanded one hundred soldiers, as the Latin name for this rank implies. However, centurions sometimes had fewer than a hundred soldiers under their command. Although centurion was a rank in the Roman army, other armies could also have centurions. ("Lieutenant" is a French word, but not everyone who holds this rank is French.) Thus the centurion whom Jesus encounters in Capernaum (Matt 8:5–13; Luke 7:1–10) was not in the Roman army but in the armed forces of Herod Antipas, the governor of Galilee. He and probably most of the soldiers under his command were Gentiles, recruited locally or from surrounding regions. They served more as Herod's police force than as a wartime army. The centurion who supervised the crucifixion of Jesus (Matt 27:54; Mark 15:44; Luke 23:47) was in the Roman army under the command of Pontius Pilate. He, too, was a Gentile, as would have been the troops he commanded.

### What did being a disciple of Jesus involve?

Generally, a first-century Jewish disciple was someone who studied for a period of time under a teacher. Once this training was complete, the disciple could in turn become a teacher, gathering disciples and passing on to them what he had learned. However, Jesus' call of men and women to follow him involved not a temporary apprenticeship but a lifelong personal relationship with him. Being a disciple of Jesus meant sharing his life and accompanying him as he traveled about, taught, and healed. Hence Jesus issued his invitations to discipleship by saying, "Come after me" (Mark 1:17) or "Follow me" (Mark 2:14). At the same time, some of those closest to Jesus did not accompany him in his travels: the Gospels portray Martha, Mary, and Lazarus as remaining at home and extending hospitality to Jesus. Matthew, Mark, and Luke generally show Jesus taking the initiative in inviting men and women to become his disciples, rather than would-be followers taking the first step toward discipleship. Becoming a disciple of Jesus could involve not only some break with one's family and livelihood but potentially even giving up one's life. That was the cost of sharing the life of the one who would lay down his life for the sake of others.

### Were elders older?

The Greek word for "elder" (*presbyteros*) literally means someone who is older (Luke 15:25), and it was used to refer to someone with authority within a family or clan, or within a group such as a synagogue or village (Luke 7:3). Religious scholars of the past could also be called elders (Mark 7:3). In the Gospels, the word "elders" usually refers to wealthy and influential Jewish laymen, particularly those who are part of the Sanhedrin in Jerusalem (Mark 15:1). In the early Church, the word "elders," or "presbyters," was used for local Church leaders (Acts 14:23), and the Greek word came through Latin into English as the word "priest."

### Who were the Essenes?

Essenes are not mentioned in the Bible. Ancient writers described them as a sect of Jews. Pliny the Elder (a Roman who lived from A.D. 23 to 79) wrote, "On the west side of the Dead Sea is the solitary tribe of the Essenes, which is remarkable beyond all the other tribes in the whole world, as it has no women and has renounced all sexual desire, has no money, and has only palm trees for company" (*Natural History,* 5:73). The first-century Jewish historian Josephus described the Essenes as celibate men who lived at the Dead Sea and owned everything in common; he added that there were also Essenes, some married, who lived throughout the land. Josephus numbered the Essenes at four thousand, several hundred of whom lived at their headquarters by the Dead Sea, in all likelihood at the site known today as Qumran. Most scholars identify the Essenes as the group who collected or wrote the Dead Sea Scrolls. Some scrolls show that the Essenes rejected the current high priests in Jerusalem as illegitimate and Temple worship as corrupt. Essenes determined religious feasts by a calendar different from the one used by the Temple. They expected God to act soon to vindicate them in a cosmic battle that would bring the end of this age; God would send two messiahs, one priestly and one royal. The Essenes carefully studied and rigorously observed the law of Moses and made daily ritual washings and communal meals part of their life. The Gospels describe no encounters between Jesus and the Essenes, but Jesus was likely aware of them. Jesus and the Essenes would have agreed that God was about to act but would have differed over how. Rome destroyed Qumran in A.D. 68, and the Essenes disappeared from history.

### How great was Herod the Great?

Two individuals are called Herod in the Gospels: Herod the Great, who ruled when Jesus was born, and his son Herod Antipas, who ruled Galilee during Jesus' public ministry. Herod the Great's father was an Idumean, a people of Edomite ancestry who had been forcibly converted to Judaism in 129 B.C. Herod the Great's mother was an Arabian princess, making Herod and his sons half-Jewish at best in the eyes of many. Herod the Great's father was an administrator employed by Rome to oversee Judea. After his father was poisoned by Jewish opponents, Rome made Herod king of Judea, Samaria, Galilee, and some territories to the east and south. Herod the Great was ambitious, shrewd, and ruthless in eliminating any who stood in his way. He undertook projects in a manner that bordered on megalomania, dotting his kingdom with palaces, massively redoing the Temple complex in Jerusalem, and building temples to the Roman emperor in other cities. He had ten wives and many children, some of whom he murdered on suspicion that they were plotting against him. Herod the Great ruled from 37 to 4 B.C. At his death, Rome divided up his kingdom among three of his sons. Archelaus was made ruler of Judea, Samaria, and Idumea, but governed so incompetently that Rome removed him in A.D. 6 and appointed Roman governors to rule his territory. Philip was given rule over a territory that lay north and east of the Sea of Galilee and included Bethsaida and Caesarea Philippi. He ruled well until his death in A.D. 33 or 34. A third son, Herod Antipas, was made ruler of Galilee and of a region east of the Jordan River.

### Who was Herod Antipas, the ruler of Galilee when Jesus lived there?

A son of Herod the Great, Herod Antipas ruled Galilee as Jesus was growing up and during his public ministry. Herod Antipas's mother, Malthace, one of his father's ten wives, was a Samaritan. After the death of Herod the Great in 4 B.C., Rome divided his kingdom among three of his sons. Herod Antipas was made tetrarch of Galilee and of a region east of the Jordan River called

Perea; he is sometimes called Herod the Tetrarch in the Gospels and sometimes simply Herod. The title "tetrarch" originally meant the ruler of a fourth part of a kingdom but later was used for a ruler who was of lesser rank than king. Herod Antipas executed John the Baptist, but Galilee was generally tranquil during his more than forty years of rule. Herod Antipas was deposed by Rome for political intrigue and exiled in A.D. 39.

## Who were the Herodians?

Herodians are mentioned three times in the Gospels (Matt 22:16; Mark 3:6; 12:13), but little is known about them other than what their name probably implies: they were supporters of the dynasty founded by Herod the Great. One of his sons, Herod Antipas, ruled Galilee and an area east of the Jordan River during Jesus' public ministry; another son, Philip, ruled the region northeast of the Sea of Galilee (see Luke 3:1). The Herodians likely included men whom Herod Antipas or Philip had entrusted with royal estates, who served as their officials, or who were in other ways dependent on them for their wealth and position. The Herodians' interests would have lain in keeping Herod Antipas and Philip in power and friendly to them. Since Herod Antipas and Philip ruled on behalf of Rome, their supporters would also have been loyal to Rome and would have favored payment of taxes. The Herodians may have hoped Rome would again place Judea under the rule of a descendant of Herod (which Rome would in fact do during A.D. 41–44).

### What were the high priest and the chief priests?

In the Old Testament the office of high priest is traced back to Aaron. Over the course of time, the high priesthood became restricted to descendants of Zadok, the high priest at the time of Solomon. This succession was broken by Syrian and Maccabean rulers in the second century B.C., when they made the office of high priest a political appointment. A small number of Jews considered these latter high priests illegitimate, since they were not descendants of Zadok. The high priest had ceremonial functions; he alone could enter the Holy of Holies of the Temple, once a year, on the Day of Atonement. The importance of the high priest extended beyond ceremonial matters. He had authority over the Temple and its income, which was the mainstay of the economy in Jerusalem. Because the high priest was the highest-ranking Jewish authority, he served as an intermediary between Rome and the Jewish people. Rome expected the high priest to help keep the nation in line and to ensure payment of tribute, or taxes, to Rome. The high priest remained in office at the pleasure of Rome. The Gospels refer to "chief priests," a group that would have included the current high priest, former high priests, other high-ranking priests and members of high-priestly families. The chief priests were a wealthy aristocracy within the priesthood. Ordinary priests carried out their assigned duties in the Temple but had little say over how it was run.

## What was the Jewish population of Palestine at the time of Jesus?

There are no records of the Jewish population of Judea and Galilee at the time of Jesus. Most modern scholarly estimates range between six hundred thousand and one million, although a few put the figure higher. Along with the Jewish population, there were a few hundred thousand Gentiles, mainly concentrated in Gentile areas and larger cities, and a smaller number of Samaritans living in Samaria. The villages of Galilee where Jesus carried out most of his public ministry were exclusively Jewish, but Jesus also traveled into some of the predominantly Gentile areas that ringed Galilee.

## Does the word "Jews" have different meanings in different Gospels?

Until the time of the Babylonian exile in the sixth century B.C., God's people were commonly referred to as Israelites, a word occurring over six hundred times in the Old Testament. After Israelites returned from exile around 538 B.C., they settled in Jerusalem and the surrounding area. This region became known as Judea because it was originally the territory of the tribe of Judah. Those living in Judea began to be called Judeans, a word that passed through Greek and Latin into English as the word "Jews." Those who shared their religious and ethnic heritage but lived outside Judea also began to be called Jews. The word "Jews" is used about one hundred seventy times in Old Testament books written after the return from exile, and about seventy-five times in the four Gospels. In the Gospels of Matthew, Mark, and Luke, "Jews" means those of Jewish birth and beliefs, as opposed to other ethnic groups. This is also the meaning of "Jews" in some instances in the Gospel of John, including where Jews are favorable to Jesus (John 8:31; 11:36, 45; 12:11). But the word "Jews" can have additional connotations in the Gospel of John, including instances where "Jews" refers to those of Jewish birth *who reject Jesus and his followers*. The parents of the man born blind were themselves Jews (of Jewish birth), yet they "were afraid of the Jews" (those of Jewish birth who reject Jesus and his followers): "His parents said this because they were afraid of the Jews, for the Jews had already agreed that if anyone acknowledged him as the Messiah, he would be expelled from the synagogue" (John 9:22). Readers of John's Gospel must discern the particular connotation the word "Jews" has in each passage of the Gospel, and not take all references to "the Jews" to signify all Jews of the time of Jesus, much less all Jews of all times.

## What were the Pharisees?

Pharisees were a group or movement, primarily of laymen, who developed particular traditions for how

God's law was to be observed. Although they were influential, they were only one group within first-century Judaism. An ancient historian reports that there were about six thousand Pharisees at the time of Jesus, out of a total Jewish population estimated by modern scholars at a half million to one million in Judea and Galilee. The Pharisees' traditions particularly spelled out how a Jew should observe the Mosaic law regarding food, tithing, the Sabbath, and ritual purity. Pharisees had their origin about one hundred fifty years before the birth of Jesus, and their rules for observing the law of Moses were handed on as "the tradition of the elders" (Mark 7:3, 5) — traditions established by earlier Pharisees. Pharisees accepted recent developments within Judaism, such as belief in an afterlife (Acts 23:6-10). Jesus' outlook was closer to that of the Pharisees than to that of any other group we know of in first-century Judaism. Sadducees, for example, denied that there would be a resurrection of the dead, while Jesus affirmed it (Mark 12:18-27). But Jesus also had some serious disagreements with the Pharisees. These disagreements carried over into the early Church, which found itself in competition with the Pharisees for the allegiance of Jews. Since the Pharisees were concerned with daily life rather than Temple worship, their influence survived the destruction of the Temple in A.D. 70, and they were among those who shaped the future course of Judaism. The Judaism of today is not identical to that of the Pharisees of the time of Jesus, but the traditions of the Pharisees are part of the roots of modern Judaism.

## Who was Philip the tetrarch?

Luke recounts that the word of God came to John the Baptist when "Herod was tetrarch of Galilee and his brother Philip tetrarch of the region of Iturea and Trachonitis" (Luke 3:1–2). A "tetrarch" was a ruler of lessor rank than a king. After Herod the Great died in 4 B.C., one of his sons, Herod Antipas, inherited rule of Galilee, and another of his sons, Philip, inherited rule of a largely Gentile territory northeast of Galilee, a region that Luke calls Iturea and Trachonitis. Herod Antipas and Philip were half-brothers, sons of Herod the Great by different mothers. Philip built a capital city for himself which he named Caesarea in honor of the Roman emperor; it became known as Philip's Caesarea — Caesarea Philippi. Bethsaida also lay within Philip's territory. Thus Jesus spent time in Philip's realm during his public ministry. Matthew and Mark recount that Philip was married to Herodias, who left him to became the wife of Herod Antipas (Matt 14:3; Mark 6:17). Philip ruled competently until his death in A.D. 34.

## What were Pontius Pilate's responsibilities?

Pontius Pilate was the Roman governor of Judea and the adjacent regions of Samaria and Idumea from about A.D. 26 to 36. His official title was prefect, or military commander, and he also carried out the duties of procurator, or civil administrator, collecting taxes. Pilate was a member of the lower Roman nobility that Rome drew on for governors of unimportant but sometimes troublesome provinces like Judea. Pilate lived in Caesarea, on the Mediterranean coast, using as his headquarters, or praetorium, a seaside palace built by Herod the Great. Paul was later held captive there (Acts 23:35). Pilate commanded about twenty-five hundred to three thousand soldiers, most of whom were stationed in Caesarea but some of whom manned the Antonia Fortress, adjacent to the Temple in Jerusalem. During Jewish pilgrimage feasts, when Jerusalem was crowded with pilgrims, Pilate and his Caesarea troops went to Jerusalem to keep order. Pilate could be quite heedless of Jewish sensitivities, and he aroused anger by bringing images of the Roman emperor into Jerusalem and by taking money from the Temple treasury to pay for an aqueduct. The Gospels portray Pilate as weak and indecisive. Philo, a first-century Jewish writer living in Egypt, might have been exaggerating when he characterized Pilate as arrogant, corrupt, cruel, and given to executing people without trial. Pilate seems to have been a man who made ill-considered decisions but backed down under pressure. He was removed as governor after his troops killed some Samaritans. The fact that Pilate kept Caiaphas as high priest during his whole term as governor indicates that the two men established a working relationship.

## How did priests and Levites differ from each other?

The office of priesthood was hereditary. All priests were members of the tribe of Levi and descendants of Aaron (Exod 28:1; 29:9; Num 18:1, 7); those who were of the tribe of Levi but not descended from Aaron served in the Temple in secondary roles as Levites (Num 1:47–53; 8:5–26; 18:2–6). At the time of Jesus there were perhaps seven thousand priests and ten thousand Levites, out of a total Jewish population in Palestine of a half million to a million. Priests in the time of Jesus were primarily responsible for offering sacrificial worship in the Temple. During the Old Testament era, priests also instructed the people in the law of Moses, but in time this function largely passed to scribes, that is, professional scholars and teachers, although some priests were also scribes. Priests from high-priestly families lived in Jerusalem and were in charge of the Temple. Most priests lived in other towns and only served in the Temple a week at a time on a twenty-four-week rotation. There was a considerable gap in income and influence between the Jerusalem high-priestly families and ordinary priests living outside Jerusalem.

## Who were the Sadducees and what did they believe?

Sadducees were an aristocratic group or party centered in Jerusalem and largely made up of high-priestly families and members of the upper class. They were an elite and hence a rather small group within Jewish society.

Sadducees were religiously conservative, upholding their own interpretation of the law of Moses and rejecting traditions developed by Pharisees. The Sadducees also rejected beliefs in a resurrection of the dead and new beliefs about angels that had arisen in the second century B.C. (see Acts 23:8). Sadducees cooperated with Roman rule in order to maintain their privileged status. Sadducees as an identifiable group did not survive the Roman destruction of Jerusalem in A.D. 70.

### What was the Sanhedrin?

At the time of Jesus, it was common for cities to have some form of city council, with what we think of as legislative, judicial, and executive responsibilities. In Jerusalem this council was called the Sanhedrin, from the Greek for "sitting together." Its members were drawn from the aristocracy of high-priestly families and wealthy, influential citizens, called elders, and included some religious scholars, called scribes (see Mark 15:1). The high priest presided over the council's deliberations. Since A.D. 6, Judea and Jerusalem had been under direct Roman rule, exercised through governors such as Pontius Pilate. Rome normally allowed subject peoples to manage their own affairs, as long as public order was maintained and taxes were paid. The Sanhedrin was the chief Jewish ruling body in Jerusalem under Roman authority. It dealt primarily with religious matters, but since religion pervaded all of Jewish life, authority in religious matters covered a wide range of concerns. The Sanhedrin's religious authority extended beyond Jerusalem because of its makeup and the importance of the Jerusalem Temple in Jewish life.

### *What did scribes do?*

The scribes encountered in the Gospels are scholars and teachers of the law of Moses, but the profession of scribe included others as well. A scribe was literally someone who could write, a literate person in a largely illiterate society. Scribes ranged from village scribes who handled routine correspondence and record keeping to high-ranking officials in governmental administrative positions. (Today we apply the title "secretary" both to a clerical assistant and to the secretary of state.) In the Gospel accounts, scribes are men who specialize in studying and teaching the law of Moses and are centered in Jerusalem. Luke sometimes uses "scholars of the law" as an alternative name for scribes. When Jesus proclaimed interpretations of the law different from those of scribes, conflicts arose between scribes and Jesus. Some scribes (a professional group) were Pharisees (a religious group), but not all scribes were Pharisees, and not all Pharisees were scribes. Some Jerusalem priests were also scribes, and some scribes were Sadducees, an aristocratic elite that included some members of the high-priestly families. After the destruction of Jerusalem by Rome in A.D. 70, some scribes took part in the reshaping of Judaism and were among those who became known as rabbis.

# 6

# WHAT COMES NEXT?

### *What is "The day of the Lord"?*

Old Testament prophecy is filled with expectations that God will act to vanquish evil. Some expectations are expressed in terms of "the day of the Lord" or "that day" or "the day when" God will act, or similar expressions. Originally "the day of the Lord" meant a time when God would vindicate his people by defeating their enemies. But Amos proclaimed that it would be a time when God would judge his own sinful people (Amos 5:18–20). Other prophets issued similar warnings, sometimes with the promise that God would restore his people after punishing them. Some prophecies use cosmic imagery to convey how momentous "the day of the Lord" would be (Isaiah 13:9–10; Joel 2:10–11; 3:3–4). Isaiah prophesied that that day would have worldwide consequences, not only restoring Israel but bringing a reign of justice to all nations (Isaiah 2:2–4; 19:18–25; 25:6–9). Most prophecies envision "the day of the Lord" as a time when God will act directly; a few prophecies portray God raising up a descendant of David to rule

God's people (Isaiah 11:10; Jer 23:5–6; 30:7–9; 33:14–18; Zech 3:8–10). "The day of the Lord" thus carries a range of meanings in the Old Testament, some of which influenced expectations of the Messiah and the establishment of the kingdom of God, although "the day of the Lord" prophecies do not use these terms. Similarly, although there are no explicit mentions of "the day of the Lord" in the four Gospels, they do reflect expectations concerning it. In the letters of the New Testament, "the day of the Lord" takes on the meaning of "the day of the Lord Jesus Christ," when he will judge the human race and establish the final reign of God (see 1 Cor 1:8; Phil 1:6, 10; 2:16).

### What significance was seen in cosmic signs?

Ancient conceptions of the universe led people to believe that events observed in the heavens carried significance for the unfolding of God's plans on earth. The universe was sometimes thought to consist of the earth under the dome of the sky (Gen 1:6–9), with sun, moon, and stars set in this dome (Gen 1:14–18). God's dwelling was imagined to be in or above the sky (Gen 28:12; Deut 26:15; 1 Kings 8:30; 2 Macc 3:39 — the Hebrew and Greek words for sky also mean "heaven"), although the heavens could not contain him (1 Kings 8:27). Stars looked small — small enough to fall from the sky as meteorites. Eclipses of the sun were known to occur. Eclipses of the moon can give it a deep red or copper hue, due to the refraction of its light by the earth's atmosphere; Joel spoke of the sun being "turned to darkness, / and the moon to blood" (Joel 3:4). Since these events happened in God's heavenly domain, they were taken as signs of God's action. Furthermore, when the prophets announced that God was going to act, as on a "day of the Lord," they sometimes used cosmic upheavals as symbolic images for God's acting (Isaiah 13:9–10; Joel 2:10–11; 3:3–4). At the time of Jesus, cosmic imagery was used to indicate that God was acting in some very significant way, but did not mean that the physical universe was coming to an end.

### What revelations of the end times were in circulation at the time of Jesus?

A number of books written in the centuries around the time of Jesus employed a distinctive type of writing, called apocalyptic, to convey a vision of God triumphing over evil. Two of these books are Daniel, in the Old Testament, and Revelation, in the New Testament; there were similar writings that were not accepted as inspired Scripture. The book of Revelation's Greek title is *Apokalypsis,* a word that means "an uncovering" or "a revelation." This Greek word is the source of the name for writings of this sort, which unveil what is hidden, characteristically employing symbols and imagery to do so. This type of writing grew out of Old Testament prophecies that described a future quite different from the present (Isaiah 24–27; 34–35; 56–66; Ezek 38–39; Joel 3–4; Zech 9–14; Mal 3). Apocalyptic writings often contain an account of a revelation given to a human being by an angel, telling what is going to happen in the future by means of symbolic accounts of events on earth and in heaven. This type of writing flowered in difficult times, when evil seemed to be winning out and the only hope was for God's intervention. Different books described different futures, but they commonly spoke of God judging and destroying the wicked, transforming this world, and beginning a new age. Those who remained faithful to God would be rewarded in an afterlife.

## What were Jewish expectations at the time of Jesus?

Jews in Palestine were ruled by Rome or by Rome's client kings, and their taxes were burdensome. The high priest served at the pleasure of Roman authority — one reason why many devout Jews, who revered the Temple, had low regard for those who controlled it. The situation Jews found themselves in fell far short of what God had promised his people through prophecy: rule by a descendant of David, an era of peace and prosperity, God manifestly dwelling in his Temple in Jerusalem, Jews returning from other lands to dwell in the land God promised to their ancestors, Gentiles either turning to the God of Israel or being subject to the rule of Israel, and God's Spirit being poured out. Any Jew who took these prophecies seriously had to be struck by the disparity between how things were and how prophecies promised they would be. Expectations were fanned by various nonbiblical writings in the two centuries before Jesus which spoke of God acting soon to set things right. Different Jewish groups envisioned different scenarios for what God would do. Some expected God to act directly; some expected God to act through one or more messiahs. Some foresaw the conversion of Gentiles to allegiance to the God of Israel; others foresaw their destruction. Some thought the end of the present age was near and that God's final triumph over evil was not far off. While there was no agreement over how God would bring an end to the unsatisfactory situation in which God's people found themselves, many shared the expectation that God would do something about it.

### What expectations were there of life after death?

For the ancient Israelites, a human being was living flesh, and meaningful life apart from the flesh was inconceivable. There was no belief in an immortal soul; the Hebrew word that is sometimes translated as "soul" can mean the livingness of a body but not something that can enjoy existence apart from a body. What survived death was at best a shadow or a ghost of one's former self, consigned to a netherworld beneath the surface of the earth (Num 16:31–33). The netherworld was a place of darkness and silence; those in the netherworld were cut off from the living and from God (Job 14:20–21; Sirach 17:22–23). Good and bad alike languished in the netherworld, sharing the same fate (Eccl 9:2–6). It was only near the end of the Old Testament era that hopes arose that there would be meaningful life after death. These hopes were often expressed in terms of bodily resurrection from the dead (2 Macc 7; Dan 12:2). However, the book of Wisdom, written around the time of Jesus, drew on Greek thinking and taught that after death, "the souls of the just are in the hand of God" (Wisd 3:1). Greek philosophers thought of souls as immortal and as temporarily imprisoned in bodies (see Wisd 9:15); death meant the release of the soul from this imprisonment. Some nonbiblical Jewish writings presumed that there would be life in the age to come but were vague about its nature.

### What was anticipated as the age to come?

Since there was no expectation of meaningful life after death in early Old Testament times, if God was to reward good and punish evil it had to be in this life. Most of the prophecies of the Old Testament share this perspective: God will rescue or punish his people through the events of history. Late in the Old Testament era a new perspective developed that is expressed in a first-century Jewish writing: "The Most High has made not one age but two" (4 Ezra 7:50 — a book not in the Bible). According to this perspective, God would bring an end to the present age and inaugurate a new age. The age to come was conceived of differently in different writings; there was general agreement that God would bring human history with all its evils to an end and reward good and punish evil at a judgment. This was often associated with God fully establishing his reign over his people and all peoples, but there were different expectations for how this would happen. Jesus spoke of the present age and the age to come (Mark 10:30; see also Luke 20:34–35) and proclaimed that the kingdom of God was at hand (Mark 1:15), which meant that the present age was drawing to an end (Matt 13:39–40, 49; 24:3; 28:20). Paul speaks of Christians as living in the present age (Rom 8:18; 12:2) and yet having been rescued from it (2 Cor 5:17; Gal 1:4): Jesus began establishing the reign of God, but we still await its fullness.

### Did Jews at the time of Jesus believe that they would face God's judgment after death?

For much of the Old Testament era, Israelites did not expect a meaningful life after death but only a shadowy existence in the netherworld for good and bad alike. As expectations arose that there would be life after death, there also arose the expectation that God would judge individuals after death, rewarding those who had led good lives and punishing those who had done evil. God's judgment is implicit in the book of Daniel, written about 164 B.C.: "Many of those who sleep / in the dust of the earth shall awake; / Some to everlasting life, / others to reproach and everlasting disgrace" (Dan 12:2). The book of Judith, written after Daniel, speaks of judgment: "The Lord Almighty will requite them; / in the day of judgment he will punish them: / He will send fire and worms into their flesh, / and they will weep and suffer forever" (Judith 16:17). In some nonbiblical writings of the era, God's judgment marks the transition between this age and the age to come. Some of these writings portray Gehenna as the place of fiery punishment.

## *What was Gehenna?*

Gehenna is a transliteration of the Greek form of the Hebrew name for the Hinnom Valley, a steep ravine on the western and southern sides of Jerusalem. In Old Testament times the Hinnom Valley was the setting for idolatrous worship (called "Ben-hinnom" — Jer 7:31; 19:1–6) which took place at sites that may have been considered entrances to the underworld. The Hinnom Valley was also used for burials and as a refuse dump. As the ideas of judgment after death and punishment of the wicked developed, some nonbiblical writings portrayed the Hinnom Valley as a place of fiery punishment, perhaps because of its smoldering refuse and associations with death and idolatry. When Jesus spoke of Gehenna as a place of everlasting punishment, he was using imagery familiar to his listeners.

## *What hope was there for a resurrection of dead at the time of Jesus?*

While there was apparently no belief in an afterlife worth living during most of the Old Testament era, various hopes for the resurrection of the dead arose in the two centuries before Jesus. These hopes were associated with expectations that God would transform the world, ending the present age and inaugurating a new one. One of the first hopes was that martyrs who had given up their lives for their faith would be raised to new life so that they could be part of God's new creation (2 Macc 6–7). The book of Daniel went a step further: not only would the righteous be raised to be part of God's reign, but the wicked would be raised as well, to be punished (Dan 12:2). How Jews conceived of resurrected bodies depended on how they conceived of God's reign in the age to come. If the age to come would be like the present age except that God would be in charge, then a person's body in the age to come would be like that person's present body (see 2 Macc 7:11, 23; 14:46). Some conceived of the age to come in less earthly terms and thought that the resurrected would have heavenly bodies, making humans like angels. At the time of Jesus, some Jews, including Pharisees, believed in the resurrection of the dead, but other Jews, including Sadducees, did not (Acts 23:6–8).

### What did Jesus teach about the kingdom of God?

The central theme of Jesus' preaching was that God was establishing his kingly rule: "The kingdom of God is at hand" (Mark 1:15). (Matthew's Gospel usually refers to it as the kingdom of heaven, reflecting the Jewish practice of avoiding using the name "God" out of reverence.) When Jesus spoke of the kingdom of God, he was invoking Old Testament images of God reigning as king (Psalm 97:1; Isaiah 52:7), and so his listeners would have had some grasp of what he was talking about. Yet the expression "the kingdom of God" never occurs in the Hebrew Scriptures and is rarely found in the New Testament except on the lips of Jesus. The coming of the kingdom of God means the coming of God's final triumph over evil; it means the coming of God's direct, manifest reign over everyone and everything. Jesus' listeners would not necessarily have understood it to mean the end of space and time, but they would at least have understood it as the end of the world as they knew it — the end of a world shot through with evil and suffering, a world in which God's people were in bondage to their sins and to foreign domination. The kingdom of God was anticipated as the fulfillment of hopes engendered by Old Testament prophecies and by nonbiblical writings of the two centuries before Jesus. But because of the richness and diversity of these prophecies and writings, Jesus' listeners had no single blueprint in mind for what the reign of God would be like. Some expected God to free them from Roman rule; others expected God to accomplish a great deal more. Jesus used parables to convey what the reign of God was like.

### What is eternal life?

The book of Daniel announces that "Many of those who sleep / in the dust of the earth shall awake; / Some to everlasting life, / others to reproach and everlasting disgrace" (Dan 12:2). "Everlasting life" is not simply life without end; those rising to be punished will also have unending life. Everlasting life (usually translated "eternal life" in English versions of the New Testament) is exalted life; those receiving it will "shine brightly / like the splendor of the firmament" (Dan 12:3). The Gospels of Matthew, Mark, and Luke identify eternal life with being saved and entering into the kingdom of God (see Matt 19:16, 23–25; 25:34, 46; Mark 10:17, 23–26; Luke 18:18, 24–26). These Gospels mention eternal life a total of eight times and speak much more often of the kingdom of God. The Gospel of John mentions the kingdom of God only twice but speaks of eternal life seventeen times; it also speaks of life nineteen times with the connotation of eternal life (for example, John 20:31). As with the other Gospels, eternal life is identified with entering into the kingdom of God (John 3:3, 5) and being saved (John 3:16–17; 10:9–10; 12:47, 50). In the Gospel of John Jesus proclaims, "Now this is eternal life, that they should know you, the only true God, and the one whom you sent, Jesus Christ" (John 17:3). "Know" has its common Old Testament connotation of immediate experience and intimacy; to know God is to be in communion with him. John's Gospel expresses this reality in terms of the disciple being in Jesus and Jesus in her or him (John 6:56; 15:4–7), as Jesus is in the Father and the Father is in him (John 10:38; 14:10–11, 20; 17:21). Eternal life is a share of God's life (see John 5:26; 6:57), given to women and men by his Son (John

1:4; 4:14; 5:21; 6:27, 51; 10:10, 28) through the Holy Spirit (see John 3:5–8; 6:63; 7:37–39).

## What is Paradise?

The word "paradise" in Hebrew and Greek is taken from a Persian word that originally meant an enclosure and came to mean a park or garden. In the Greek translation of the Old Testament, the "garden in Eden" is literally the "paradise in Eden" (Gen 2:8); similarly, in Isaiah "the garden of the LORD" is literally "the paradise of the LORD" (Isaiah 51:3). In some Jewish non-biblical writings, Eden became an image for an idyllic life with God after death — a life in paradise. In one of these writings, the *Psalms of Solomon,* those who love God and obey his commandments will inherit a life of happiness in "the Lord's paradise," while sinners are consigned to Hades. The word "paradise" is used once in the Gospels (Luke 23:43), once by Paul (2 Cor 12:4), and once in Revelation, where it is translated as "garden" by the *New American Bible*: "To the victor I will give the right to eat from the tree of life that is in the garden of God" (Rev 2:7). There was no single coherent view of the afterlife at the time of Jesus; paradise was one image for what we think of as heaven.

# 7

# JESUS

## Was Jesus Born "Before Christ"?

Jesus was born during the reign of Herod the Great (Matt 2:1; Luke 1:5), who died in 4 B.C. Since Herod ordered the slaughter of all Bethlehem boys two years and younger to get rid of Jesus (Matt 2:16), it is likely that Jesus was almost two at the time, indicating that he was born around 6 B.C. (The division between B.C. and A.D. dates from the sixth century, but a miscalculation made then of the year of Jesus' birth gave rise to the anomaly of Jesus being born B.C. — "Before Christ.") The available evidence indicates that Jesus was baptized by John and began his public ministry around A.D. 28 when he was about thirty-four years old, and that he was crucified around A.D. 30 when he was about thirty-six. This means that Jesus spent most of his adult life as a carpenter in Nazareth.

## What kind of work did Jesus do as a carpenter?

The Greek word *tekton*, used to describe Jesus (Mark 6:3) and Joseph (Matt 13:55), is usually translated carpenter. A *tekton*, however, worked not just with wood but with any hard and lasting material, including stone. Houses in Nazareth usually had unworked stone walls; wood was used sparingly for roof beams, doors, and door frames. Jesus spoke of building on rock (Matt 7:24) and laying a cornerstone (Mark 12:10), and he might have had firsthand experience of doing both. A *tekton* would also have been expected to have the skills to make and repair plows, yokes, and furniture. Our mental image of Jesus the carpenter should be of a skilled manual laborer.

### What did Jesus look like?

Neither the Gospels nor any other New Testament writing describes what Jesus looked like. Artists through the ages have generally portrayed him as looking like the people of their own culture. Yet Jesus assuredly looked like a person of his own culture, a first-century Galilean Jew. His fellow citizens in Nazareth found him so ordinary that they had trouble accepting him as anything more than the village carpenter. Yet his being a carpenter does provide some evidence about him. Whether he was tall or short, stocky or sinewy, he was strong. As a carpenter he worked with stone as well as wood. Wooden beams and sometimes stone blocks were cut and shaped with hand tools; a man who spent his life working as a carpenter would have callused hands and hard muscles. If the Shroud of Turin is authentic (and this is debated), then it indicates that Jesus was almost six feet tall, weighed about one hundred and seventy five pounds, was right-handed, and had a beard and long hair.

### What languages did Jesus speak?

The language of ancient Israel was Hebrew, and most of the Old Testament was written in Hebrew. Jesus would have had to have a reading knowledge of Hebrew in order to read aloud from the scroll of Isaiah in the synagogue in Nazareth (Luke 4:16–21). Aramaic, a related language, was the international language of the Babylonian and Persian empires. Jews adopted Aramaic as their ordinary language after the Exile, when they were under the rule of Persia. Some chapters of the books of Ezra and Daniel, written during or after this period, are in Aramaic. Jesus grew up speaking Aramaic, the ordinary language of Jews in Palestine in the first century. The Gospels preserve a few Aramaic words that Jesus used, such as *talitha koum* (little girl, arise — Mark 5:41) and *Abba* (Father — Mark 14:36). Following the conquests of Alexander the Great around 330 B.C., Greek became widely used throughout the eastern Mediterranean world, especially for commerce. Scholars debate whether Jesus knew any Greek. The common view is that he probably picked up some Greek words but taught in Aramaic, the language in which both he and the rural people of Galilee were most at home.

## What does it mean that Jesus is the Son of David?

Broadly speaking, any descendant of David could be called a son of David (as Joseph is — Matt 1:20). The Messiah was commonly expected to be a descendant of David (Matt 22:42; Mark 12:35; Luke 20:41; John 7:42) and therefore could be called the Son of David. While the Old Testament provides ample basis for such expectation, no Old Testament passage uses the title "Son of David" as a title for the Messiah. The Messiah is, however, called the Son of David in one of the *Psalms of Solomon*, a nonbiblical writing from around 50 B.C. It is striking that during Jesus' public ministry, others call him the Son of David only in conjunction with his healings (Matt 9:27; 12:23; 15:22; 20:30–31; Mark 10:47–48; Luke 18:38–39. Matt 21:9 may not be an exception: see Matt 21:14–15). There is evidence that popular Jewish tradition looked upon Solomon, a son of David, as an exorcist and a healer, and some scholars suggest that Jesus was hailed as the Son of David during his ministry because he, too, exorcised and healed. Matthew proclaims Jesus to be the Son of David who is the Messiah (Matt 1:1, 16–7). Luke's Gospel makes it explicit that Jesus is the descendant of David through whom God's promise of an everlasting reign for the house of David will be fulfilled (2 Sam 7:12–16; Psalm 89:3–5, 29–38; Luke 1:32–33).

## Why did Jesus refer to himself as the Son of Man?

Jesus uses the expression "Son of Man" more than eighty times in the four Gospels; it is found only four times in the rest of the New Testament. In its origin it is a Hebrew and Aramaic idiom that means "human being." Psalm 8 uses "a son of man" as a synonym for "man": "What is man that you are mindful of him, / and a son of man that you care for him?" (Psalm 8:5). Ezekiel is repeatedly addressed by God as "son of man" (Ezek 2:1; 3:1; 4:1, etc.). Jesus employs the expression as a way of referring to himself during his public ministry, even when he is doing things that by human standards are extraordinary, for example, forgiving sins (Mark 2:10). In other passages, Jesus uses the expression "Son of Man" when speaking of his coming suffering and death. In still other passages, Jesus refers to himself as the Son of Man when speaking of himself as risen and returning in glory at the end of time. These last instances echo the use of "One like a son of man" in Daniel 7:13–14. Neither in Daniel nor in any other Jewish writing from before the time of Jesus is "Son of Man" used as a title for the Messiah. Jesus' referring to himself as the Son of Man was distinctive: others did not call him the Son of Man. It is also enigmatic: scholars have endlessly debated the complexities of this title.

### What does it mean that Jesus is the Son of God?

The title "son" (or "sons") "of God" carries a variety of meanings in the Old Testament. It is applied to angels and members of the heavenly court (Job 1:6; 2:1; 38:7). It is used to refer to the people of God (Exod 4:22; Deut 14:1). A king in the line of David could be referred to as a son of God (2 Sam 7:14; Psalm 2:7), as could a devout Israelite (Wisd 2:18). It is not, however, a title explicitly associated with the Messiah: no prophecy refers to the Messiah as the Son of God. When the title "Son of God" is applied to Jesus in the Gospels or in Paul's letters, it carries a far greater meaning than in the Old Testament, since it refers to Jesus' unique relationship with God as his Father. This is particularly developed in the Gospel of John. Paul focuses on what Jesus is able to do to bring us salvation because he is the Son of God (Rom 5:10; 8:3, 32; Gal 4:4–5; Col 1:13). In later centuries, the Church reflected on what Jesus' sonship meant in terms of his divinity. The Council of Nicaea in A.D. 325 proclaimed that the "Lord Jesus Christ, the Son of God" is "true God from true God, begotten not made, consubstantial with the Father" — another translation is "one in Being with the Father." The Council of Chalcedon, held in A.D. 451, proclaimed that Jesus Christ is one person with two natures, a divine nature and a human nature, so he is both fully divine and fully human.

### *What is the significance of Jesus calling upon God as "Abba, Father" (Mark 14:36)?*

While God is called or called upon as Father in some books of the Old Testament, such occurrences are infrequent and generally refer to God as the Father of his

Israelite people rather than the father of an individual. In marked contrast there are about one hundred seventy occurrences in the Gospels of Jesus speaking of or praying to God as his Father; it is the characteristic way that Jesus speaks of or with God. Mark's Gospel indicates that Jesus used the Aramaic word *abba* in addressing God as his Father (Mark 14:36). *Abba* is an informal and colloquial word for "father," a word children used in speaking to their fathers, using it even after they had become adults. There is no exact English equivalent for *abba;* perhaps the closest is "Dad." Jesus' addressing and speaking of God as his *Abba* reflects the unique intimacy Jesus enjoyed with him and his consciousness of being the Son. Yet Jesus authorized his disciples to address his Father as their Father, teaching them to pray "Father" (Luke 11:2) or "Our Father" (Matt 6:9). There is evidence that Jesus taught his disciples to also pray to God as their *Abba,* for this was the practice even among Christians whose native language was not Aramaic. Paul, writing in Greek to Greek-speaking Christians, referred to their calling upon God as *Abba:* "God sent the spirit of his Son into our hearts, crying out, 'Abba, Father!'" (Gal 4:6; see also Rom 8:15). Followers of Jesus are to share in his intimacy with his Father.

### What does it mean that Jesus is the Messiah, the Christ?

There is a tendency to define the title "Messiah," or "Christ," in terms of who Jesus is, and to presume that this is the meaning that the word *messiah* had for Jews at the time of Jesus. The situation was more complex, however. The Hebrew word *messiah* is a noun meaning "anointed one," that is, a person anointed, or smeared, with oil — usually olive oil. Israelite kings were ceremonially anointed, as were high priests. Thus a king could be referred to as God's "anointed" (Psalm 2:2). Based partly on a prophecy of the prophet Nathan, an expectation developed that an anointed descendant of David would play a decisive role in God's plans for his people. Nathan prophesied to David that his throne would "stand firm forever" (2 Sam 7:16), but David's dynasty came to an end with the Babylonian conquest of 586 B.C., and Jews were under foreign rule for the next four centuries. In the two centuries before Jesus, there was a resurgence of hopes for rule by a descendant of David — a messiah. Alongside various expectations for a kingly messiah, nonbiblical Jewish writings from this period spoke of other messianic figures; there was no single, clearly defined picture of a messiah. One Jewish group, the Essenes, expected God to send two messiahs: a kingly messiah descended from David and a priestly messiah descended from Aaron. Most messianic hopes had a political dimension: God would bring an end to Roman domination. Some expected God to bring the present age to an end and to usher in a new age. There was no expectation that a messiah would suffer: the "servant" of Isaiah 52:13—53:12 was not identified with the Messiah before the time of Jesus.

Jesus was ambivalent about being called the Messiah. On the one hand, he could accept it, because he *was* God's agent establishing the reign of God. On the other hand, popular understandings of what a messiah would do usually included the overthrow of Roman rule, and that was not Jesus' mission. Jesus clarified what it meant for him to be called the Messiah through his teachings, death, and resurrection. The New Testament, written in Greek, uses the Greek word for "anointed," *christos,* which gives us the word "Christ." The early Church embraced the word "Christ" as its most common title for Jesus, so much so that it evolved from being a title (Jesus the Christ) to being virtually a second name (Jesus Christ).

### What does it mean that Jesus is a savior?

A savior is someone who rescues others from danger or death. Throughout the Old Testament God is spoken of as the savior of his people (Exod 15:2; 1 Macc 4:30; Isaiah 43:3). God also raised up individuals as saviors (Judges 3:9; 15; Neh 9:27). Jesus rescues from death by giving eternal life, making him a savior (Luke 2:11), "the savior of the world" (John 4:42). The New Testament speaks of both God and Jesus as saviors: "God our savior ... Christ Jesus our savior" (Titus 1:3–4).

### What are the implications of calling Jesus Lord?

The Greek word for "lord" is *kyrios,* familiar to many in the form in which it occurs in the petition *Kyrie, eleison* (Lord, have mercy) — Greek words in the Roman liturgy. A *kyrios*, or lord, has wide application to someone who has power and authority. The owner of a property could be called its *kyrios* (the "owner of the vineyard" in Mark 12:9). A master would be addressed as "lord" by his servants. And anyone could use "lord" as a polite form of address to a man, much as the English word "sir" is used (see John 12:21). At the other extreme, Greek-speaking Jews used the word *kyrios* — "Lord" — as a title for God, as did New Testament writers (Luke 1:32; Rev 1:8). Because of this range of usage, when Jesus is called *kyrios* by someone in the Gospels, it may simply be a respectful form of address (translated as "sir" in John 4:19), an acknowledgment that he is someone with authority (the meaning of "Lord" in Matt 8:21 and Luke 7:6), or a declaration that he is "Lord" as God is "Lord" (the meaning of "Lord" in John 20:28 and Phil 2:11).

### What does an Advocate do?

Both Jesus and the Holy Spirit can be called an Advocate. Jesus implicitly refers to himself as an Advocate when he promises to send his disciples "another Advocate to be with you always, the Spirit of truth" (John 14:16–17). The first letter of John also refers to him as an Advocate, proclaiming that "we have an Advocate with the Father, Jesus Christ the righteous one" (1 John 2:1). Yet we think primarily of the Holy Spirit as the Advocate. In John's Gospel, Jesus during his public ministry speaks of men and women being born of water and Spirit (3:3–8) and of the Spirit enabling proper worship to be offered to God (4:23–24). During his last supper with his followers he addresses what the Spirit will do for them after he returns to the Father. In the Greek of John's Gospel, Jesus calls the Spirit a *parakletos*, transliterated as "Paraclete," which the *New American Bible* translates as "Advocate." The Greek word means "called alongside" and signifies someone who is called to one's side to assist. In a legal setting, a *parakletos* was an advocate or witness for an accused person. A *parakletos* was not a defense attorney (such did not exist in ancient courts) but someone who took the side of the accused, testifying on their behalf and perhaps assailing the prosecution. While the word Paraclete aptly characterizes the Spirit as being with the followers of Jesus to assist them, the Gospel of John infuses the title with greater meaning. The coming Paraclete or Advocate will continue the work that Jesus began while he was on earth. In particular, just as Jesus is the truth (14:6), the Advocate is the Spirit of truth who brings to mind what Jesus taught (14:17, 26) and guides his followers into a fuller understanding of his revelation (16:13–15).

### Who was responsible for Jesus' death?

Along with the four Gospels, two other ancient writings help determine responsibility for Jesus' death. The

Roman historian Tacitus (who lived from about A.D. 56 to 118) wrote that Christ "had been put to death by the procurator Pontius Pilate during the reign of Tiberius." The Gospels indicate that the notice posted on the cross charged Jesus with being "the King of the Jews" (Matt 27:37; Mark 15:26; Luke 23:38; John 19:19) — an insurrectionist. Jesus was executed in the manner that Rome used to get rid of insurrectionists: crucifixion. At the time of Jesus, only Romans, not Jews, could crucify. Jesus died at Passover, when Jerusalem was filled with pilgrims. A city seething with religious and nationalistic fervor could generate sparks of revolt, and Pilate apparently treated Jesus as such a spark, crucifying him. The Jewish historian Josephus (who lived from about A.D. 37 to 100) wrote that Pilate, "upon hearing him accused by the men of the highest standing among us," condemned Jesus to be crucified. Pilate acted at the urging of the high priest and his associates. They controlled the Temple, which was the source of their power and income. Jesus disrupted commerce in the Temple precincts, upsetting those in charge (Mark 11:15–18; John 2:14–18). More ominously, Jesus spoke about the Temple being destroyed (Mark 13:1–2; John 2:19). Religious disagreements certainly led some people to oppose Jesus. But those who were personally responsible for his death were a Roman governor bent on maintaining order and religious leaders whose status depended on the Temple. The Second Vatican Council stated, "Even though the Jewish authorities and those who followed their lead pressed for the death of Christ (John 19:6), neither all Jews indiscriminately, nor Jews today, can be charged with crimes committed during his passion" (*Nostra Aetate,* 4).

# PALESTINE AT THE TIME OF JESUS

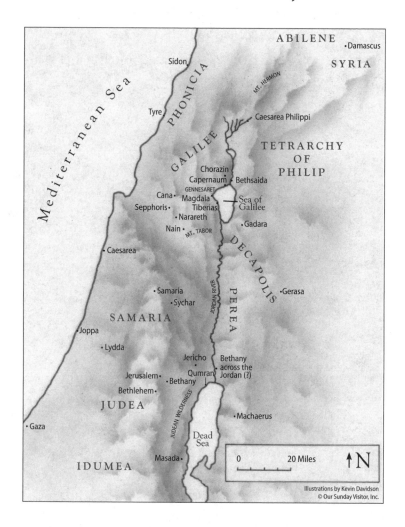

Illustrations by Kevin Davidson
© Our Sunday Visitor, Inc.

# JERUSALEM AT THE TIME OF JESUS

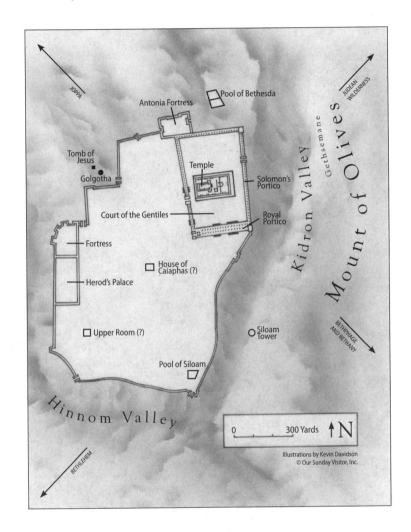

# INDEX OF KEY WORDS